D0914893

What The BIBLE really says about Marriage, Divorce and Remarriage

EDWARD G. DOBSON

What The BIBLE really says about Marriage, Divorce and Remarriage

Fleming H. Revell Company
Old Tappan, New Jersey

Scripture quotations in this book are from the King James Version of the Bible.

Chart taken from *Helping Children of Divorce* by Judson J. Swihart and Steven L. Brigham. © 1982 by Inter-Varsity Christian Fellowship of the USA and used by permission of Inter-Varsity Press, P.O. Box 1400, Downers Grove, IL 60515.

Material from J. S. Wallerstein and J. B. Kelly, "The Effects of Parental Divorce," *American Journal of Orthopsychiatry* 46 (2) April 1976. Reprinted, with permission, from the *American Journal of Orthopsychiatry*. Copyright © 1976 by the American Orthopsychiatric Association, Inc.

Excerpts from *Relationships in Marriage and the Family* by Nick Stinnett, James Walters, and Evelyn Kaye reprinted with permission of Macmillan Publishing Company. Copyright © 1977 by Macmillan Publishing Company

Library of Congress Cataloging-in-Publication Data

Dobson, Ed.

What the Bible really says about marriage, divorce, and remarriage.

Bibliography: p.

1. Marriage--Biblical teaching. 2. Divorce--Biblical teaching. 3. Remarriage--Biblical teaching. I. Title.

BS680.M35D63 1986 241'.63 86-22050

ISBN 0-8007-1493-8

Published by the Fleming H. Revell Company

Old Tappan, New Jersey 07675

Printed in the United States of America

Contents

	Foreword by Tim LaHaye	7
	Introduction	9
Chapter One	**The Essentials of Marriage**	15
Chapter Two	**Divorce and the Teaching of Moses**	32
Chapter Three	**Divorce and the Old Testament**	42
Chapter Four	**The Teachings of Jesus**	53
Chapter Five	**Divorce and the Teaching of Paul**	70
Chapter Six	**Divorce and the Church**	83
Chapter Seven	**The Bible, Human Sexuality, and Adultery**	94
Chapter Eight	**Children, Single Parents, and Divorce**	106
Chapter Nine	**The Family: Building on the Right Foundation**	135

Chapter Ten **Summary and Overview** 158
Questions and Answers 163
Bibliography and Further Reading 185

Foreword

Everything Ed Dobson does is quality. This book is no exception. In addition, its perspective is biblical, practical, and very timely.

It was my intention to skim the book and then write the Foreword, but I became so intrigued by it, I read every word. He writes in a fascinating style and has the ability to express himself logically.

I cannot exaggerate how important I believe this book is. There is not a church in the nation, nor very many families, not touched by divorce. As a counselor I know few things that cause more emotional pain—not only to the couple, but also to their children, parents, and grandparents. I am sorry to say, divorce will be with us from now on into the twenty-first century. We Christians seem to tag along behind the world's practices about a decade—so we also are now feeling the rash of divorce the secular society experienced about a decade ago. I would say divorce is three times more prevalent in the church today than it was ten years ago.

With such an increase in this tragedy, there has been a host of attempts to cope with it, all the way from ignoring the problem to extreme legalism that is unforgiving. One produces licentiousness and the other extreme frustration.

Divorce is not the end of the world. And although the

church needs to oppose divorce and do all we can to help couples from going through it, we should not treat divorced persons as lepers or second-rate citizens.

Much of the advice I have heard Christians (and even some ministers) give is based either on humanistic thinking or religious prejudice. We need to get back to what the Bible teaches on this, so we can help people pick up the pieces of their lives and go on with God.

I am convinced there is a "perfect, acceptable and good will of God" (*see* Romans 12:2) for every Christian. For those who miss the "perfect will of God" through divorce, we in the church should know what the Bible really says about their situation so we can help them move on to the "acceptable will of God" for their life. I have met some who, on the contrary, give personal opinions that banish them to a lifetime of loneliness or make them think divorce is just like any other sin. It is not! Marriage is one of life's most significant decisions; therefore, the decision to terminate that marriage is equally as significant—and they both bear lifetime consequences.

This book may not be the last word on divorce from a biblical perspective, but it will come close. Dr. Dobson analytically shows what the Bible really says, compares Scripture with Scripture, and deals with all the difficult problems, like remarriage, sin, the double standard (does God have a different standard for Christian leaders than for lay people?), the attitude of the church, and so forth.

Every minister, divorced man or woman, or Christian interested in knowing what the Bible says about this problem can be helped by reading this book. It is not only biblically accurate, it is tenderly compassionate.

TIM LAHAYE
President,
Family Life Seminars

Introduction

I was sitting on the platform next to Dr. Jerry Falwell at Thomas Road Baptist Church. As the teacher of the Pastor's Bible Class, I was about to embark on a new series of messages entitled "Marriage, Divorce, and Remarriage." I sat there that morning waiting to speak, and the longer I waited, the more nervous I became. I knew that the messages I would give over the next ten weeks would be highly controversial. In fact, several of the pastors in our church and professors at the university advised me not to teach on the subject of divorce. They felt I would only further divide the congregation and alienate people. As I sat and waited, I was beginning to think that I should have taken their advice. *Why generate controversy anyway?* I thought. *I could be teaching a safe verse-by-verse exegesis of some book.*

Why had I chosen to deal with divorce? First of all, I felt impressed of the Lord to address the subject from a biblical perspective. I had never studied the subject in detail (although I had been quick to give my opinion when asked). Second, I knew that many people in our congregation were dealing with the separation and divorce of friends and neighbors, and as such, needed some source of biblical direction. Third, I was convinced that divorce was becoming a major problem within the church and that in many cases the church and the clergy were hiding their heads in the sand. I felt it was time to deal with the issue head-on.

Soon it was time to speak. A few minutes into the message, my fears and anxieties were gone, and I was consumed with the responsibility of teaching God's Word. I survived the series. There was not any division or controversy—not that everyone agreed with my interpretations. In fact, during one lesson I made the statement, "Now, not everyone will agree with my interpretation," and from the congregation a person responded with a loud "Amen"—loud enough for all four thousand people to hear! One pastor even collected the tapes from members of his congregation and had them burned because he felt they promoted error. (The messages were so well received that Dr. Falwell had put them into a cassette package and offered them to our television and radio audience.) The response was overwhelming. Over 140,000 people requested the tapes, and I have received hundreds of letters from people all over the world.

This book is the outgrowth of these messages and the letters, questions, and advice I have received from others. I have tried to struggle with each of the texts that relate to marriage and divorce. I do not claim infallibility and I freely acknowledge both my bias and limitations. I am a pastor—not a scholar. I am interested in relating biblical truth to the problems of contemporary society. I am not interested in writing in language that only a few professors can understand. While the title of the book *What the Bible Really Says About Marriage, Divorce, and Remarriage* may sound presumptuous, that is certainly not the intent. I am confident that before this book is published, someone will raise questions that I have not addressed.

Many will not agree with me—that's fine. I shall never forget one of the first letters I received in response to the tapes:

> Why on earth would Jerry Falwell have a character like you teaching about marriage, divorce, etc.?
>
> Evidently you and your wife are ex'es and you are trying to salve your conscience.

> You're all wet. May God in heaven save your poor soul before it is too late and you have misled souls to eternity.
>
> My first thought was to return your tapes, but to prevent other damage, I will destroy them.

My only objective is to force you to stand before God's Word. I have tried not to appeal to other authorities—whether Murray, Adams, or Ryrie. I have tried only to ask, "What does the Bible teach?"

As I write this Introduction I feel the same fears and anxieties that I did that Sunday morning at Thomas Road Baptist Church—the fear of being misunderstood—the fear of being rejected—the fear of being wrong. But we must not allow our fears to inhibit us from addressing the tough issues of life. My prayer is that this book will strengthen the family, discourage divorce, and at the same time give hope and encouragement to separated and divorced Christians.

EDWARD G. DOBSON
June, 1986

What The BIBLE really says about Marriage, Divorce and Remarriage

Chapter One

The Essentials of Marriage

Divorce has come a long way in our society! From a time when it was never considered an option—even under the worst circumstances—it gradually moved into an era when it was considered a disgraceful choice. Still, only the most brazen and rebellious brought this shame to their families. Over time, however, divorce became tolerable, the lesser of evils in certain situations. Finally, the stigma of divorce faded, and soon people began to encourage divorce as an easy and desirable alternative to the difficult task of solving marriage problems.

Now people divorce merely as a matter of course or convenience. Many never consider marriage a lifetime commitment. Divorce has become part of the plan—always an available out.

Not Just a Secular Problem

Not only is divorce a problem of society in general, it is a problem of the church in particular. Who can say he has no friends or relatives affected by divorce? I remember twenty-two years ago when our family emigrated to the United States, and my father became a pastor of a church in the Philadelphia area. Shortly after assuming the pastorate, a married couple came to my father for counseling. They were in the process of getting a divorce. I remember how their situation shocked the entire congregation. Back then, it was extremely rare for Christians to divorce and it was considered tangible evidence of failure on their part. Now twenty years later things have changed. When I taught this series on divorce at Thomas Road Baptist Church, I asked the congregation to indicate if they knew a close friend or relative who recently divorced or was going through a divorce. The response was overwhelming. Almost every person in the four thousand-member class knew a close friend or relative going through the trauma of divorce. Christians are not immune to family breakup.

As twentieth-century Christians, we face the problem of determining where we will make our stand on this disturbing divorce continuum—where we will draw our line, and find a biblical resting place. And the progression of opinion as to what is right, wrong, acceptable, tolerable, understandable, disgraceful, or forbidden is every inch as long as the one divorce has run through society. With pastors and Bible scholars debating their diverse opinions, and each couple feeling their situation is exceptional, the divorce rate has tripled in the last twenty years.

As a pastor, I am faced with the dilemma of divorce almost every day. While it is relatively safe to hide behind the ivory towers of scholarship and make *ex cathedra* pronouncements about divorce, it is infinitely more difficult to apply the truth of Scripture to the lives of hurting and suffering people. Every person is different, and every situation is different. I will not attempt to deal with every possible separation and divorce situation—such would require many more volumes. Rather, I will attempt to identify overarching biblical principles that transcend the specific details of every situation. I believe it is our responsibility to take these principles, and with prayer, love, and sensitivity, apply them to the complexities of the issue of divorce and remarriage.

What Are the Basic Principles of Marriage?

Before we can begin discussing divorce, we must have a clear understanding of the essential nature of marriage. What is a marriage? In order to answer that question, let us study the first marriage and discover God's creative intent when He established and sanctioned that marriage. Liberal theologians have often argued that if Christians would just give up the first twelve chapters of Genesis, our Christianity would be more palatable to the intelligentsia-elite of the secular world. But we cannot do that. The first twelve chapters of Genesis are foundational for the rest of God's revelation. That is certainly true when you consider the subject of marriage. What God intended for Adam and Eve is what God intends for us in the twentieth century. While time, people, and cultures change, the demands of God for humanity do not change.

In the early chapters of Genesis we discover five fundamental principles of marriage.

1. God Created Male and Female.

> And God said, Let us make man in our image, after our likeness: and let them have dominion over the fish of the sea, and over the fowl of the air, and over the cattle, and over all the earth, and over every creeping thing that creepeth upon the earth.
>
> So God created man in his own image, in the image of God created he him; male and female created he them.
>
> Genesis 1:26, 27

Someone has said, "God created Adam and Eve—not Adam and Steve!" In the beginning God created man and woman—

separate but equal, similar but distinct. Society's movement toward a unisex concept of men and women is contradictory to God's creative intent. Society's increasing acceptance of homosexual and lesbian marriages as legitimate is in clear violation of Scripture. Men and women are different physically and emotionally. These differences must be recognized and accepted as ingredients for a successful marriage.

2. *God Recognized the Need for Companionship.*

> And the Lord God said, It is not good that the man should be alone; I will make him an help meet for him.
>
> 2:18

The word *help* is the Hebrew word *'ezer,* meaning "a supporter." The word does not imply inferiority—that God created man and then woman; therefore women are to help and support men as servants would. The same Hebrew word is also used in reference to God Himself—He is our helper, our support in time of difficulty.

For instance, in Exodus 18:4 we find that one of Moses' sons was named Eliezer—*el* is the Hebrew word for *God* and *'ezer* is the word for *support. Eliezer* means "God our supporter."

The word is used in Psalms 33:20. "Our soul waiteth for the Lord: he is our *help* and our shield" (italics added). It is used in Psalms 146:5. "Happy is he that hath the God of Jacob for his *help,* whose hope is in the Lord his God" (italics added). God is a helper to all of us, and because He *is* God He is in no way inferior to us. God created woman to be a helper *but this in no way implies she is inferior to man.* This idea of equality is further emphasized in the phrase, ". . . I will make him an *help meet* for him" (Genisis 2:18). This could also be translated, "I will make a supporter corresponding to him."

The idea that woman was made for man and man for woman is clearly observed in the sexual relationship.

> Let the husband render unto the wife due benevolence: and likewise also the wife unto the husband.
>
> The wife hath not power of her own body, but the husband: and likewise also the husband hath not power of his own body, but the wife.
>
> Defraud ye not one the other, except it be with consent for a time, that ye may give yourselves to fasting and prayer; and come together again, that Satan tempt you not for your incontinency.
>
> 1 Corinthians 7:3–5

Paul reminds us that our bodies belong to our partners. Mutual submission in the sexual relationship brings true fulfillment in the marriage relationship.

3. *God Established the Basic Guidelines of Marriage.*

> Therefore shall a man leave his father and his mother, and shall cleave unto his wife: and they shall be one flesh.
>
> And they were both naked, the man and his wife, and were not ashamed.
>
> Genesis 2:24, 25

These verses are the Magna Carta of marriage. They contain the essential elements for understanding the nature of marriage and they articulate the fundamental concepts for making a marriage successful. Verse 24 is repeated four times in the Bible and is quoted by Jesus Himself when dealing with the issue of marriage and divorce. However, there is some controversy about who actually made this statement in Genesis 2:24. Some people believe Adam said it. However, since Adam did not have a father or a mother, he probably would not say he had left them. Other people believe that Moses, under divine inspiration of the Holy Spirit, added these words when describing the first marriage. I believe these are the words of God Himself.

Notice the context in which they are spoken. In verses 21 and 22 the formation of Eve is described. Taking a rib from Adam, God creates a woman and brings her to Adam. The Talmud comments on the significance of this creative act. "God did not create woman from man's head that he should command her, nor from his feet that she should be his slave, but rather from his side that she should be near his heart." In verse 23, Adam responds to God's gift with a song of praise. "And Adam said, This is now bone of my bones, and flesh of my flesh: she shall be called Woman, because she was taken out of Man." Then the guidelines for marriage are given in verses 24 and 25. I believe that these are the words of God Himself as He establishes His standards and guidelines for marriages. Four guiding concepts are found in verses 24 and 25.

Separation. A man is to "leave" his father and mother. This word means to "abandon, give up, or leave behind." That does not mean that once you get married you no longer have a relationship with or a responsibility to your parents. We have an obligation to honor our parents. But God says that once you marry, you leave the authority of your father and mother. You leave that family unit and become a family of your own. There must be a clear line of separation. Failure in this area is one of the underlying causes for divorce. I have counseled with many distressed couples who were victims of the control of their parents. Sometimes the parents were at fault, and sometimes the couples themselves could not cut the apron strings. As much as we ought to love, respect, and honor our parents, there must be a clear and definite separation from them at the time of marriage. Couples who marry and then move into one of their parents' houses are destined for problems and may be sowing the seeds of destruction for their relationship.

Cleaving. The Hebrew word used here means "to be glued together." In the context of marriage it implies the cementing together of two people into one relationship. This word is used in Job 38:38. "When the dust groweth into hardness, and the clods *cleave* fast together" (italics added). This verse is speaking of how dust is glued together into mud after a rainstorm. In 2 Kings 5:27, Elisha told his servant, "The leprosy therefore of Naaman shall *cleave* unto thee, and unto thy seed . . ." (italics added). Now that does not mean that getting married is like contracting leprosy! The idea is that marriage is permanent—as was the disease of leprosy during Old Testament times. Since leprosy was incurable, once a person contracted it there was no way to get rid of it. The leprosy was "glued" to the person. As leprosy "cleaves" to the body permanently, so marriage is the binding together of two people into a permanent relationship. Marriage is more than separating from mother and father—it is a bonding together of two people.

Paul reminded the church of Colossae that it is love which binds the church together.

> Put on therefore, as the elect of God, holy and beloved, bowels of mercies, kindness, humbleness of mind, meekness, longsuffering;
>
> Forbearing one another, and forgiving one another, if any man have a quarrel against any: even as Christ forgave you, so also do ye.
>
> And above all these things put on charity, which is the bond of perfectness.
>
> Colossians 3:12–14

What is true of the church is true of the family. Love is the glue which binds together the husband and wife. In dealing with couples who are going through separation and divorce, I have frequently heard one or both of them say, "I don't love my spouse anymore." When love begins to die, the marriage begins to come apart.

Becoming one flesh. Although this refers primarily to sexual union (1 Corinthians 6:16), a careful study of how the word *flesh* is used in the Old Testament reveals the concept of more than merely a physical union. It is a "oneness" of mind, emotions, will, spirit, and physical being. It is "oneness" of person. In Genesis 6:17 this word is used to describe people—not just physical bodies. "And, behold, I, even I, do bring a flood of waters upon the earth, to destroy all *flesh,* wherein is the breath of life, from under heaven; and everything that is in the earth shall die" (italics added). Notice the progression—separation, cleaving, one flesh. Husband and wife become one person with one mind and one direction. Have you ever noticed that people who have been married for many years start to look and act like each other? That's the idea here.

Shamelessness. "And they were both naked, the man and his wife, and were not ashamed." Few commentators mention the significance of this statement as it relates to marriage. Adam and Eve had an open, transparent, vulnerable relationship. They had nothing to hide. Marriage therefore should involve an openness and transparency. Although this concept has been marred by the entrance of sin, it is nevertheless an important ingredient for a strong and healthy relationship in marriage.

4. *God Intended a Permanent Relationship.*

> And he answered and said unto them, Have ye not read, that he which made them at the beginning made them male and female,
>
> And said, For this cause shall a man leave father and mother, and shall cleave to his wife: and they twain shall be one flesh?

> Wherefore they are no more twain, but one flesh. What therefore God hath joined together, let not man put asunder.
>
> Matthew 19:4–6

God's original intention was that the marital relationship be a permanent, lifelong agreement. When Jesus repeated the marriage formula given in Genesis 2:24, He added an additional phrase. He stated, "What therefore God hath joined together, let not man put asunder" (Matthew 19:6). Although Moses outlined concessions for divorce within the Jewish community, that was not God's original intent. The vows of the Episcopal marriage ceremony emphasize this point.

> I ________, take thee________, to my wedded Wife, to have and to hold from this day forward, for better for worse, for richer for poorer, in sickness and in health, to love and to cherish, *till death do us part,* according to God's holy ordinance; and thereto I plight thee my troth (italics added).

Numerous passages in the Bible emphasize the permanence of the marital relationship.

> Know ye not, brethren, (for I speak to them that know the law,) how that the law hath dominion over a man as long as he liveth?
>
> For the woman which hath an husband is bound by the law to her husband so long as he liveth; but if the husband be dead, she is loosed from the law of her husband.
>
> Romans 7:1, 2

> The wife is bound by the law as long as her husband liveth; but if her husband be dead, she is at liberty to be married to whom she will; only in the Lord.
>
> 1 Corinthians 7:39

As we discuss the biblical guidelines for divorce and remarriage, it is critical to keep in mind that God's ultimate will is *one man, for one woman, for one lifetime.* That is still God's ideal design for the twentieth-century marriage.

Does the Husband Rule Over the Wife?

The principles of Genesis 2:24, 25 were established before sin entered the world. After Adam and Eve sinned, God outlined different roles within the marriage relationship: "Unto the woman he said, I will greatly multiply thy sorrow and thy conception; in sorrow thou shalt bring forth children; and thy desire shall be to thy husband, and he shall rule over thee" (3:16). Two specific statements are made in regard to the marital relationship. First, the wife's "desire" will be to her husband and second, the husband will "rule over" his wife. What do these statements mean? Some people translate the first part in the following manner: "And thy desire shall be *against* thy husband." They suggest that the inclination of the woman will be to resist and rebel against the male leadership of her husband. Because of this rebellion, the husband must then "rule over" (manage) his wife. *I disagree with this interpretation.* Rebellion against God's authority is inherently a part of our fallen human nature. Men and women are both equally rebellious. To suggest that because of the Fall there is an antithetical battle of the sexes that requires the domination of the male species is to suggest something that is not explicitly taught in Scripture.

This text does, however, outline different roles and functions in the marital relationship. The husband is to exercise spiritual leadership in the home. There is equality of person in marriage, but there is a difference of function. This principle is also found in 1 Corinthians 11:3: "But I would have you know, that the head of every man is Christ; and the head of the woman is the man; and the head of Christ is God." Christ is co-equal with the Father in all matters pertaining to deity, yet this verse tells us that God is the head over Christ. In the Trinity there are differences of function and purpose, but there is equality of person. *So it is in marriage.* The husband and wife have different functions, but neither is inferior or superior to the other. The so-called Christian feminists argue that the submission of the wife was the curse of the Fall, and that Christ died to deliver us from that curse. Therefore, in Christ there is neither male or female and that the Old Testament idea of female submission is no longer applicable. However, these feminists fail to address the clear teaching of Paul in Ephesians 5:22, 23, "Wives, submit yourselves unto your own husbands, as unto the Lord. For the husband is the head of the wife, even as Christ is the head of the church: and he is the saviour of the body."

In Figure 1, I have outlined the chain of authority that is accepted by many Christians. Notice that the woman is to be completely submissive to the man. Some would even suggest that if the husband asks his wife to do something wrong, she should obey him, and that he will be totally accountable to God for the sin of his wife. For example, if the husband asks his wife to lie for him or give sexual favors to his boss, she should do it. Such unconditional obedience is unscriptural. Everyone is responsible to God for their behavior! In Figure 2, I have outlined what I believe to be the appropriate chain of authority within the home. This will be discussed in greater detail in chapter 9.

What Is a Biblical Marriage?

Exactly what is a marriage? Marriage is not "living together" or engaging in sexual relations. When Jesus told the woman at the well to call her husband, she replied that she had no husband. She was living with a man to whom she was not married. Jesus said, "Thou hast well said, I have no husband: for thou hast had five husbands; and he whom thou now hast is not thy husband." Although she was living with a man and presum-

Figure 1
THE UNCONDITIONAL CHAIN OF COMMAND

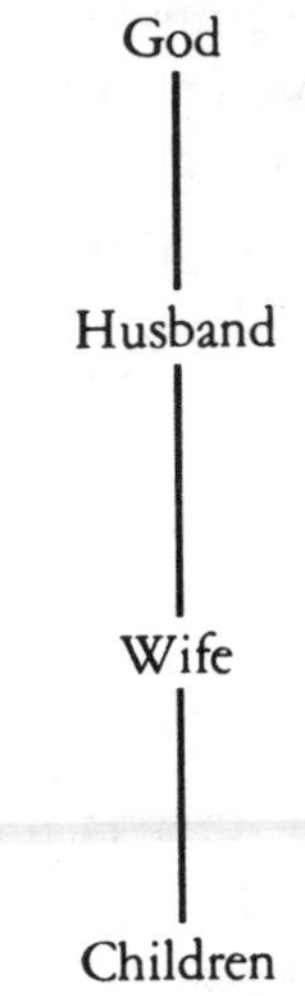

Figure 2
THE SCRIPTURAL CHAIN OF COMMAND

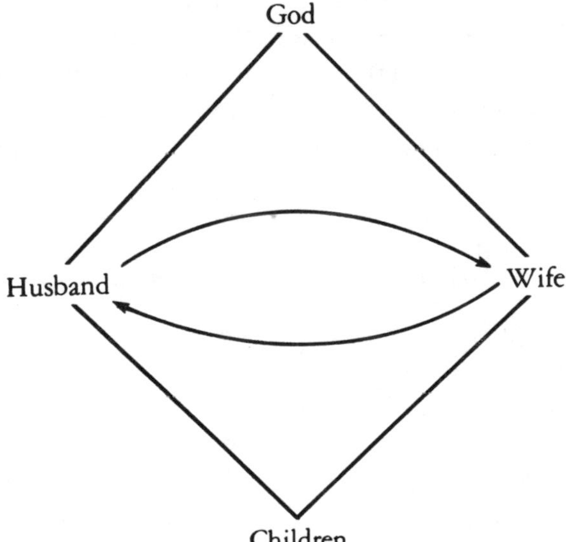

ably engaging in sexual activity, she was not married to him. Jesus makes this clear. In the eyes of God, *living together does not constitute a marriage.*

What then is a marriage? Marriage is a "covenant of companionship." It involves both a convenantal relationship and a companionable relationship.

1. Marriage Is a Covenant.

> Which forsaketh the guide of her youth, and forgetteth the covenant of her God.
>
> Proverbs 2:17

> Yet ye say, Wherefore? Because the Lord hath been witness between thee and the wife of thy youth, against whom thou hast dealt treacherously: yet is she thy companion, and the wife of thy covenant.
>
> Malachi 2:14

In Proverbs 2:17, the writer is dealing with a prostitute who has forsaken the marital relationship. She has forgotten "the covenant of her God." That is, she has forgotten her marital covenant. In Malachi 2:14, the wife is called the "wife of thy covenant." In Old and New Testament times marriage was a covenant made between two people and witnessed by God. According to Webster, a covenant is a "binding and solemn agreement made by two or more individuals, parties, etc. to do or keep from doing a specified thing." The Hebrew word for covenant is *berith,* which many believe is derived from the Hebrew verb *barah,* which means "to cut" (*see* Genesis 15:17, 18). It carries the idea of an agreement made between two parties that binds them to privileges and obligations. It is an agreement uniting people in mutual obligations. In biblical times this covenant was made at the time of engagement (known as betrothal). This agreement, made by the parents of the bride and groom, united both parties in mutual obligations.

In Genesis 24:58, 60, we are given an example of the formula for blessing that accompanied the betrothal.

> And they called Rebekah, and said unto her, Wilt thou go with this man? And she said, I will go.
>
> And they blessed Rebekah, and said unto her, Thou art our sister, be thou the mother of thousands of millions, and let thy seed possess the gate of those which hate them.
>
> Genesis 24:58,60

The parents of the bride were given a dowry as part of the covenant. This could be in the form of money, land, or even services rendered (Genesis 29). The covenant guaranteed the ensuing marriage ceremony and the relationship could only be broken during the engagement period by serving another legal document—a bill of divorcement. This is illustrated clearly in Matthew 1.

> And Jacob begat Joseph the husband of Mary, of whom was born Jesus, who is called Christ.
>
> So all the generations from Abraham to David are fourteen generations; and from David until the carrying away into Babylon are fourteen generations; and from the carrying away into Babylon unto Christ are fourteen generations.
>
> Now the birth of Jesus Christ was on this wise: When as his mother Mary was espoused to Joseph, before they came together, she was found with child of the Holy Ghost.
>
> Then Joseph her husband, being a just man, and not willing to make her a public example, was minded to put her away privily.
>
> But while he thought on these things, behold, the angel of the Lord appeared unto him in a dream, saying, Joseph, thou

> son of David, fear not to take unto thee Mary thy wife: for that which is conceived in her is of the Holy Ghost.
>
> And she shall bring forth a son, and thou shalt call his name JESUS: for he shall save his people from their sins.
>
> Now all this was done, that it might be fulfilled which was spoken of the Lord by the prophet, saying,
>
> Behold, a virgin shall be with child, and shall bring forth a son, and they shall call his name Emmanuel, which being interpreted is, God with us.
>
> Then Joseph being raised from sleep did as the angel of the Lord had bidden him, and took unto him his wife.
>
> Matthew 1:16–24

Matthew 1 records that Joseph and Mary had already made that covenant when Joseph discovered that Mary was pregnant. Being a just man, he thought about "putting her away," which is the technical term utilized to describe divorce. Once the covenant had been made, even prior to the marriage, a bill of divorcement was required to break the engagement.

2. Marriage Is a Covenant of Companionship.

> . . . she is thy companion, and the wife of thy covenant.
>
> Malachi 2:14

> And the Lord God said, It is not good that the man should be alone; I will make him an help meet for him.
>
> Genesis 2:18

The Hebrew word *companion* used in Malachi 2:14 comes from a verb which means "to tame a wild animal." That conjures up many implications for marriage! That does not mean that the responsibility of the husband is to tame his wife or the wife to tame her husband. The idea is that you can get close to a tamed animal. The fear of that animal has been removed. Marriage likewise involves the removal of fear and all other obstacles that would prohibit the building of a warm and intimate relationship. Jay Adams, a prominent Christian counselor, has said, "A companion is one with whom you are intimately united in thoughts, goals, plans, and efforts." It is the same idea as becoming "one flesh."

In Ezekiel and Ruth we have the only two passages in Scripture that refer to a marriage ceremony, or more correctly, the engagement ceremony. "Now when I passed by thee, and looked upon thee, behold, thy time was the time of love; and I spread my skirt over thee, and covered thy nakedness: yea, I sware unto thee, and entered into a covenant with thee, saith the Lord God, and thou becamest mine" (Ezekiel 16:8).

This passage portrays the groom coming and covering the bride with his garments as an indication that he is going to take her under his wing, protect her, and meet her needs. Marriage is a husband and wife making a covenant to live together as companions until death parts them.

Conclusion

We have established the fact that marriage is a covenant of companionship. Consequently, divorce must then be the breaking of that covenant of companionship. In fact, the very definition of marriage suggests the two major problems that can lead to divorce. First, *there is a lack of commitment to the original agreement.* I have found in talking with many couples who are separating that they lack a serious commitment to their marital vows and therefore have little desire to resolve their present conflicts. Second, *a loss of the intimacy, communication and concern that are inherent in the concept of companionship can lead to divorce.* How often I have heard the statement. "I just don't love him

[her] anymore!" What about divorce? Does God allow for the covenant of companionship to be broken? If so, on what grounds? We will begin exploring these and other questions in the next chapter.

Chapter Two

Divorce and the Teaching of Moses

When a man hath taken a wife, and married her, and it come to pass that she find no favour in his eyes, because he hath found some uncleanness in her: then let him write her a bill of divorcement, and give it in her hand, and send her out of his house.

And when she is departed out of his house, she may go and be another man's wife.

And if the latter husband hate her, and write her a bill of divorcement, and giveth it in her hand, and sendeth her out of his house; or if the latter husband die, which took her to be his wife;

Her former husband, which sent her away, may not take her again to be his wife, after that she is defiled; for that is abomination before the Lord: and thou shalt not cause the land to sin, which the Lord thy God giveth thee for an inheritance.

Deuteronomy 24:1–4

In the first chapter we established that marriage is a covenant of companionship—the bonding together of two people in a lifelong relationship. God's ideal for the permanency of marriage has not changed. As Christians we have every reason to stay together, because Jesus Christ can and should be the center of the marriage relationship. Divorce is not a legitimate option for Christians. In the Old Testament God commanded permanence in marriage (Genesis 2:24, 25). However, in Deuteronomy 24, He established guidelines for divorce.

The instructions on divorce in Deuteronomy 24 in no way indicate that God *commanded* divorce, rather that He *conceded* to divorce in certain circumstances, giving guidelines to control a problem that was evident even before the Pentateuch was written. In the New Testament Jesus reemphasizes the fact that God did not command divorce, rather He permitted it. The Pharisees approached Jesus to discuss the controversy of divorce and asked the question, "Why did Moses then *command* to give a writing of divorcement, and to put her away?" (Matthew 19:7 italics added). Jesus answered by saying, "Moses because of the hardness of your hearts *suffered* you to put away your wives: but from the beginning it was not so" (v. 8, italics added). Notice the different words. The Pharisees spoke of divorce as being *commanded,* while Jesus speaks of divorce being *permitted.*

What Is the Basis for Divorce in the Old Testament?

> When a man hath taken a wife, and married her, and it come to pass that she find no favour in his eyes, because he hath found some uncleanness in her: then let him write her a bill of divorcement, and give it in her hand, and send her out of his house.
>
> Deuteronomy 24:1

What was the Old Testament premise, or grounds, for divorce? If a man found uncleanness (the Hebrew word literally means "shame, disgrace, or nakedness") in his wife, he could divorce her. Many people believe this uncleanness is adultery, but it cannot be. In Deuteronomy 22:13–21 the case of a man who married a woman who had premarital relationships with other men is presented. Notice that if the woman is proven guilty, she is given the death penalty. The penalty for premarital sex after the covenant had been agreed upon was not divorce. It was death.

> Then they shall bring out the damsel to the door of her father's house, and the men of her city shall stone her with stones that she die: because she hath wrought folly in Israel, to play the whore in her father's house: so shalt thou put evil away from among you.
>
> 22:21

In verse 22 of the same chapter we read of the penalty for extramarital sex. In that case also, the penalty for adultery was death, not divorce.

> If a man be found lying with a woman married to an husband, then they shall both of them die, both the man that lay with the woman, and the woman: so shalt thou put away evil from Israel.
>
> v.22

What is the uncleanness in Deuteronomy 24? That question became the center of controversy for hundreds of years. In fact, by the time of Christ, the Jewish scholars were divided into two camps regarding their interpretation of the word *uncleanness.* The conservative school of Shammai believed a man must not divorce his wife unless he had found her unfaithful. By the time of Christ, they were no longer stoning or killing people for adultery, so these conservative Jewish rabbis believed that the only grounds for divorce was unfaithfulness in the marriage bond.

The school of Hillel was much more liberal. They believed this uncleanness referred to anything displeasing to the husband. In the first part of the Talmud, the Jewish civil and religious law, some grounds for divorce according to the school of Hillel were: violation of the Law of Moses or of Jewish customs, such as the woman causing her husband to eat food on which a tithe had not been paid; not setting apart the first dough; appearing in public with disheveled hair; spinning and exposing her arms in public; conversing indiscriminately with men; speaking disrespectfully of her husband's parents in his presence; brawling in the house; or spoiling a dish for him. These women got only one chance—if they burned supper, spoke too loudly, or wore short-sleeved garments, they were asking for a bill of divorcement!

By the time of Jesus, the Jewish community was divided over the interpretation of "uncleanness" as the grounds for divorce. In Matthew 19 the Pharisees attempt to bring Jesus into this controversy by forcing Him to take sides.

> The Pharisees also came unto him, tempting him, and saying unto him, Is it lawful for a man to put away his wife for every cause?
>
> Matthew 19:3

What are the Pharisees asking? They are asking Jesus if He subscribes to the interpretation of Hillel—divorce for "every cause."

What does the Bible mean by *uncleanness?* The word comes from a verb meaning "to be bare or empty." It is used figuratively in the Old Testament to speak of a disgrace or a blemish. Several times it is used to describe shameful exposure of the human body.

> And Ham, the father of Canaan, saw the nakedness of his father, and told his two brethren without.
>
> And Shem and Japheth took a garment, and laid it upon both their shoulders, and went backward, and covered the nakedness of their father; and their faces were backward, and they saw not their father's nakedness.
>
> Genesis 9:22, 23

> Neither shalt thou go up by steps unto mine altar, that thy nakedness be not discovered thereon.
>
> Exodus 20:26

> Jerusalem hath grievously sinned; therefore she is removed: all that honoured her despise her, because they have seen her nakedness: yea, she sigheth, and turneth backward.
>
> Lamentations 1:8

Therefore we know that uncleanness does not refer to trivial things like burning a dish or talking too loudly. It is a serious word. I believe it indicates some type of serious, shameful, and disgraceful conduct associated with sexual activity, but less than adultery.

The Scriptures indicate that there are certain intimate acts that accompany sexual intercourse. These would include the exposure and fondling of one another's bodies.

> I said, I will go up to the palm tree, I will take hold of the boughs thereof: now also thy breasts shall be as clusters of the vine, and the smell of thy nose like apples;
>
> And the roof of thy mouth like the best wine for my beloved, that goeth down sweetly, causing the lips of those that are asleep to speak.
>
> Song of Solomon 7:8, 9

His left hand should be under my head, and his right hand should embrace me.

8:3

Perhaps the "uncleanness" of Deuteronomy refers to this type of intimate physical-sexual behavior. To define the word more precisely and name specific behaviors would only be speculative.

What Was the Procedure for Divorce?

When a man hath taken a wife, and married her, and it come to pass that she find no favour in his eyes, because he hath found some uncleanness in her: then let him write her a bill of divorcement, and give it in her hand, and send her out of his house.

Deuteronomy 24:1

What was typical Old Testament divorce procedure? The Hebrew word for *divorcement* means "a cutting off," which carries with it the idea of breaking the marriage covenant. Marriage was established by a formal legal covenant, and a formal legal document was required to dissolve marriage. The custom of writing letters of divorcement was probably adopted by the Israelites when they were in Egyptian bondage. As far as we know, the Egyptians were the first civilization to demand that all legal transactions be in writing. This is an example of an ancient, Jewish, divorce document.

On the____________day of the week in the month____________ in the year____________from the beginning of the world, according to the common computation in the province of____________, I, ____________the son of____________by whatever name

I may be known, of the town of____________ with the entire consent of mind and without any constraint, have divorced, dismissed, and expelled thee,____________ daughter of____________by whatever name thou art called, of the town____________who hast been my wife hitherto; but now I have dismissed thee____________, daughter of____________by whatever name thou art called, of the town of____________so as to be free at thine own disposal, to marry whomsoever thou pleasest, without hindrance from anyone, from this day for ever. Thou art therefore free for anyone (who would marry thee). Let this be thy bill of divorce from me, a writing of separation and expulsion according to the law of Moses and Israel.

____________, the Son of____________, Witness
____________, the Son of____________, Witness

The International Standard Biblical Encyclopedia, ed. James Orr, II, p. 863, 4

There were three steps to a divorce. The husband was (1) *to write the wife a bill of divorcement,* (2) *put it in her hand,* and (3) *send her out of his house* (Deuteronomy 24:1).

The divorce procedure was intended to protect the wife. In ancient civilization women were second-class citizens. In the heathen cultures around the children of Israel, women were bought, sold, and traded like animals. The bill of divorcement that God established in Deuteronomy 24 actually protected the woman and released her from further domestic obligations. After the bill was presented and she was sent out, she was no longer obligated to any domestic responsibilities in that home. She was also free from interference by her former husband in any subsequent marriages. Finally, we have learned from the Talmud and Jewish interpretations of various writings, she was awarded financial protection. The custom was that the husband who divorced his wife was to return her dowry and give her a portion of his own estate equal to that dowry. She left the marriage with twice the lands, property, or money she brought to the marriage.

What Are the Prohibitions Against Divorce?

> And when she is departed out of his house, she may go and be another man's wife.
>
> And if the latter husband hate her, and write her a bill of divorcement, and giveth it in her hand, and sendeth her out of his house; or if the latter husband die, which took her to be his wife;
>
> Her former husband, which sent her away, may not take her again to be his wife, after that she is defiled; for that is abomination before the Lord: and thou shalt not cause the land to sin, which the Lord thy God giveth thee for an inheritance.
>
> Deuteronomy 24:2–4

What prohibitions were associated with Old Testament divorce? After divorce there was *no* prohibition against remarriage—with one exception. The wife could not be divorced from her second husband and return to her first husband. Even if her second husband died, she could not return to the first because she was "defiled." The word defiled refers to "moral, religious, or ceremonial pollution." In the Old Testament this word is used to describe the grossest types of sexual immorality and idolatry. Such a thing was an abomination unto the Lord.

Since remarriage was allowed, why was going back to the first husband considered an abomination unto the Lord? God gave this prohibition to ensure that marriage was not reduced to wife-swapping, thus defiling the very meaning and covenant of marriage. No one could say, "I'll go marry someone else, and if that doesn't work, I'll go back to my first mate." God intended that the sanctity of marriage be maintained. Is this stipulation valid for today? (This question will be answered in detail later.)

By the time of Christ, the Jews had developed guidelines for remarriage. These guidelines are from the Mishna, the Jewish interpretation of Old Testament Scriptures. They are not binding but they are interesting.

After the wife had been divorced, she was to wait three months before remarrying. She could not marry the man with whom she was suspected of having an adulterous relationship, and she was not allowed to marry the man who delivered the bill of divorcement into her hand. (For further information see G. Edwin Bontrager, *Divorce and the Faithful Church,* Herald Press, 1978.)

What Are the Principles of Divorce?

On the basis of the information we have studied in Deuteronomy 24, we can establish several important biblical principles that relate to the subject of divorce.

1. *Divorce was man-made.* God instituted marriage; He did not institute divorce. God instituted guidelines for controlling it. God commanded permanence in marriage; He conceded to grounds for divorce.

2. *Divorce was permitted on the grounds of sexual misconduct that was less than adultery.*

3. *Divorce required a legal document, breaking the marriage covenant to the same degree that death breaks the marriage covenant.*

4. *Remarriage was permitted.*

5. *The divorced person was not allowed to return to the first husband after remarriage.*

6. *Divorce provided moral and financial protection to the woman.*

7. *God commands permanence in marriage.* That is God's ideal. But in the context of Deuteronomy 24, He conceded to

divorce. These principles can be reduced to three basic concepts: *God commands permanence in marriage. God permits divorce. God permits remarriage.* These fundamental concepts are clearly taught in the Pentateuch. Whether you believe in divorce in the New Testament or not, you must conclude that in the Old Testament it was permitted along with remarriage.

Chapter Three

Divorce and the Old Testament

In chapter 2 we discussed the Mosaic guidelines for divorce as given in Deuteronomy 24. Although this is the primary Old Testament passage dealing with divorce, there are a number of other texts that merit analysis and discussion. In this chapter we will look at them.

Is All Divorce Sin?

There are some who argue that divorce is always an act of sin and, based on Matthew 19:9, is the equivalent of committing adultery. Some would further argue that anyone who remarries is living in a continual state of adultery. We will deal with these questions in detail under the teaching of Jesus. However, I want to address an important question in light of Old Testament teaching. Is all divorce sin?

> They say, If a man put away his wife, and she go from him, and become another man's, shall he return unto her again? shall not that land be greatly polluted? but thou hast played

> the harlot with many lovers; yet return again to me, saith the Lord.
>
> Jeremiah 3:1

> Thus saith the Lord, Where is the bill of your mother's divorcement, whom I have put away? or which of my creditors is it to whom I have sold you? Behold, for your iniquities have ye sold yourselves, and for your transgressions is your mother put away.
>
> Isaiah 50:1

In Jeremiah God compares His relationship with Israel to that of a couple who have been divorced. According to the Law of Moses, after the divorce the wife could not return to her original husband after she had married another. Neither can Israel return after committing spiritual adultery with the false gods of pagan religion.

> Go and proclaim these words toward the north, and say, Return, thou backsliding Israel, saith the Lord; and I will not cause mine anger to fall upon you: for I am merciful, saith the Lord and I will not keep anger for ever.
>
> Jeremiah 3:12

In Isaiah, God is reminding the children of Israel that they have forsaken Him. Although He has every right to divorce them and sell them to their creditors, He has not done so. He still loves them. However, there is the underlying threat in these words that He could write Israel a bill of divorcement. If the act of divorce is a sin, then why would God utilize this as an analogy of His relationship to Israel? Further, why would God threaten Israel with a bill of divorcement? Since God cannot sin, then the answer to these questions is that the act of divorce is ***not*** an act of sin. However, the root cause for all divorce is sin. Notice Isaiah 50:1, ". . . . Behold, for your iniquities have ye sold yourselves, and for your transgressions is your mother put away." Not all divorce is sin but the root cause of all divorce is sin.

Does God Ever Command Divorce?

> Now when these things were done, the princes came to me, saying, The people of Israel, and the priests, and the Levites, have not separated themselves from the people of the lands, doing according to their abominations, even of the Canaanites, the Hittites, the Perizzites, the Jebusites, the Ammonites, the Moabites, the Egyptians, and the Amorites.
>
> For they have taken of their daughters for themselves, and for their sons; so that the holy seed have mingled themselves with the people of those lands: yea, the hand of the princes and rulers hath been chief in this trespass.
>
> And when I heard this thing, I rent my garment and my mantle, and plucked off the hair of my head and of my beard, and sat down astonied.
>
> Ezra 9:1–3

> Now when Ezra had prayed, and when he had confessed, weeping and casting himself down before the house of God, there assembled unto him out of Israel a very great congregation of men and women and children: for the people wept very sore.
>
> And Shechaniah the son of Jehiel, one of the sons of Elam, answered and said unto Ezra, We have trespassed against our God, and have taken strange wives of the people of the land: yet now there is hope in Israel concerning this thing.
>
> Now therefore let us make a covenant with our God to put away all the wives, and such as are born of them, according to

the counsel of my lord, and of those that tremble at the commandment of our God; and let it be done according to the law.

Ezra 10:1–3

"When I heard this thing, I rent my garment and my mantle, and plucked off the hair of my head and of my beard, and sat down astonied."

Who was so confounded that he literally began to pull his hair out? Ezra. What was the problem that led to his amazed condition? Mixed marriages.

After the southern kingdom of Judah had spent seventy years in the Babylonian Captivity, approximately fifty thousand Jews returned to Jerusalem to rebuild the temple. A second group of Jews returned about eighty years later under the leadership of Ezra.

After only four months in Jerusalem, Ezra was shaken by the problems caused by many Jewish people marrying the heathen from tribes around the city. Mixed marriages were forbidden by Mosaic Law. Intermarriage ultimately led to adopting heathen worship and would lead the children of Israel into idolatry. But perhaps the major reason for the prohibition is found in Ezra 9:2: "For they have taken of their daughters for themselves, and for their sons: so that the holy seed have mingled themselves with the people of those lands. . . ." The "holy seed" is a reference to the line of the Messiah, established when God promised Abraham that through his seed all the nations of the earth would be blessed. That was possible because through the seed of Abraham ultimately came the Messiah, and the Messiah provided salvation not only to the Jews, but also to the Gentiles.

But when the Jewish remnants returned to Jerusalem and began to intermarry with heathen nations, their national identity was jeopardized, and the line of the Messiah was in danger of extinction. Ezra understood this critical situation, and this led to a plan to resolve the problem. In Ezra 10 we read that the people repented and decided to right their wrong. Revival had come.

When people speak of revival today, they say that if God sends revival, the divorce rate will go down. But in Ezra's day the Jews had revival, and the divorce rate went up!

In Ezra 10:3 the people agreed to "make a covenant with our God to put away all the wives, and such as are born of them, according to the counsel of my lord, and of those that tremble at the commandment of our God; and let it be done according to the law."

The phrase "put away" does not imply a legal separation. The Hebrew verb is the same verb used in Deuteronomy 24:2 where it clearly refers to divorce.

Did the people divorce their wives merely on the whim of Ezra, or did God command it? The small *l* in "lord" in Ezra 10:3 leads some to suggest that the speaker, Shechaniah, is respectfully calling Ezra "lord," but that would be illogical. Shechaniah would use this word only in reference to a sovereign king. I believe Shechaniah is saying, "This is not according to the word of Ezra, but according to the Word of God Himself, the King of kings, and Lord of lords."

Ezra told the people to sever their relationships with the heathen women and children. This was a difficult task, and a three-month investigation was launched to see that everything was done according to the laws of divorcement.

What were the results? They discovered that 17 priests, 10 Levites, and 86 laymen had intermarried with the nations around them. They wrote out 113 bills of divorcement.

What principle can we learn from this? First, we know they divorced their wives at the command of God. Many liberals argue that this passage teaches that there is deep-seated racism in the Jewish community. These people believe that the Jews were so prejudiced that this drastic action was taken unnecessarily.

On the other hand, others use this passage to justify or rationalize someone else's situation. Some use it to justify divorce if someone has married out of the will of God. Some apply it to a saved/unsaved combination, saying that you have every right to divorce an unbeliever and remarry a believer. Some even argue that the real problem in Ezra was incompatibility. They were from two different cultures, religions, and backgrounds; therefore divorce is allowable on the basis of incompatibility.

I do not believe this passage is proof for any of these arguments. What does it teach? Simply this: These were special one-time circumstances. The Messianic line was in jeopardy of extinction, and God commanded severe, drastic action. If some claim this passage as justification for divorce, I would like to remind them that the Messiah has already come, and therefore these circumstances cannot be repeated. But we do learn that in at least this situation, God did something more than concede to divorce. In this instance He even commanded divorce.

Does God Desire Reconciliation for Separated and Divorced People?

If you are considering separation or divorce, then you should study the life story of the prophet Hosea. Here is the story of a husband who loved in spite of his circumstances, and who refused to give up hope of reconciliation with his adulterous wife.

> The beginning of the word of the Lord by Hosea. And the Lord said to Hosea, Go, take unto thee a wife of whoredoms and children of whoredoms: for the land hath committed great whoredom, departing from the Lord.
>
> Hosea 1:2

> And I will not have mercy upon her children; for they be the children of whoredoms.
>
> 2:4

And she shall follow after her lovers, but she shall not overtake them; and she shall seek them, but shall not find them: then shall she say, I will go and return to my first husband; for then was it better with me than now.

For she did not know that I gave her corn, and wine, and oil, and multiplied her silver and gold, which they prepared for Baal.

vv. 7, 8

Then said the Lord unto me, Go yet, love a woman beloved of her friend, yet an adulteress, according to the love of the Lord toward the children of Israel, who look to other gods, and love flagons of wine.

So I bought her to me for fifteen pieces of silver, and for an homer of barley, and an half homer of barley:

And I said unto her, Thou shalt abide for me many days; thou shalt not play the harlot, and thou shalt not be for another man: so will I also be for thee.

3:1–3

God commanded Hosea to do a strange thing—take a wife of "whoredoms," a prostitute. Apparently she had some type of spiritual or conversion experience, and Hosea and Gomer were married. Gomer came to this relationship with hope for a new beginning and a totally new life. Hosea brought to that relationship the integrity of God's prophet. A son was born to the couple, and God commanded that he be called Jezreel, which means "judgment."

The firstborn son is a reminder of God's judgment on the children of Israel. I am sure that when Jezreel was born Hosea thought, *Here is the key to building a great relationship. I know my wife has had a dark past, but somehow this little baby will bring love, closeness, unity, and consistency into our family.* Soon a second child was born, Loruhamah, which means "unpitied." A third child soon followed, and God said, "Call his name Loammi" which means "not my people."

Here we have the first indication of the problems of Gomer. The words "not my people" imply that perhaps this child, or even all of Hosea's children, are not his children at all, but the results of the adulterous relationships of Gomer.

Later Hosea learns that none of these children are his and the marriage begins to fall apart. Gomer leaves. She goes from one lover to another. Hosea's embarrassment is incomprehensible as he seeks to call a nation to repentance. People say, "Why don't you straighten out your own home before telling me what to do?" His reputation is hurt. His ministry suffers. He is alone at home, trying to be a mother and father to three children who are not even his. Here is a man who had every reason to divorce his wife—but he does not.

Gomer is soon living with a man who cannot provide for her, and Hosea finds a way to sneak money to her. She does not know the money comes from Hosea, and the prophet watches in dismay as his money is taken and offered to Baal. Is he lacking in common sense? Love does not make sense. Hosea loves Gomer, and he is determined not to give up on her. Finally Gomer ends up with a lover who tries to sell her at the slave market.

From what we understand of slavery in the Old Testament, she was stripped naked and stood before a gazing crowd. Many people wanted to see Gomer get what she deserved. She had embarrassed the prophet. She had made a mockery of the family. She had hurt Hosea's reputation.

The crowd was stunned when Hosea joined them. Then someone murmured, "This is his moment of triumph and glory. He is going to see his adulterous wife sold into slavery." The bidding began—five pieces of silver, ten pieces. Then a strong voice from the back of the crowd said, "Fifteen pieces." It was Hosea.

The crowd thought, *He is going to buy her back in ultimate humiliation.* The price rose. Finally the prophet cried out, "Fifteen pieces of silver and a bushel and a half of barley." He had bought back his wife.

Why? To punish her? No. Hosea said, "Thou shalt abide for me many days; thou shalt not play the harlot, and thou shalt not be for another man: so will I also be for thee." Here is a story of unconditional love. Here we find that true love does not give up. This is also the story of God, who loves us in spite of our sin.

Whenever I am talking to people considering divorce, I always say, "Have you tried, as Hosea did, to do all you can with the love of God to reconcile your situation?" As long as there is a God in heaven capable of supernatural intervention, there is always hope. Even when you have biblical grounds for divorce, you ought to love and forgive and seek to keep your marriage together.

Are There Special Restrictions on Divorce for Spiritual Leaders?

They shall not take a wife that is a whore, or profane; neither shall they take a woman put away from her husband: for he is holy unto his God.

A widow, or a divorced woman, or profane, or an harlot, these shall he not take: but he shall take a virgin of his own people to wife.

Leviticus 21:7, 14

Neither shall they shave their heads, nor suffer their locks to grow long; they shall only poll their heads.

Neither shall any priest drink wine, when they enter into the inner court.

> Neither shall they take for their wives a widow, nor her that is put away: but they shall take maidens of the seed of the house of Israel, or a widow that had a priest before.
>
> And they shall teach my people the difference between the holy and profane, and cause them to discern between the unclean and the clean.
>
> Ezekiel 44:20–23

The priests were prohibited from marrying a widow, a divorcée or a prostitute. These requirements were not enforced upon the general population—only the priests. Because of their special calling and mission, God placed more stringent obligations upon them.

Ezekiel outlines the reasons for these stipulations. "And they shall teach my people the difference between the holy and profane, and cause them to discern between the unclean and clean." The priests represented God's holiness and in their marital relationships they were to demonstrate God's ideal. We learn an important principle from this. God places greater demands upon spiritual leaders than upon anyone else. We will study this principle in greater detail when we examine the requirements for pastors and deacons in the New Testament Church.

Does God Hate Divorce?

> Yet ye say, Wherefore? Because the Lord hath been witness between thee and the wife of thy youth, against whom thou hast dealt treacherously: yet is she thy companion, and the wife of thy covenant.
>
> And did not he make one? Yet had he the residue of the spirit. And wherefore one? That he might seek a godly seed. Therefore take heed to your spirit, and let none deal treacherously against the wife of his youth.

> For the Lord, the God of Israel, saith that he hateth putting away: for one covereth violence with his garment, saith the Lord of hosts: therefore take heed to your spirit, that ye deal not treacherously.
>
> Malachi 2:14–16

God hates "putting away" (that is, divorce). God does not hate people who are divorced. God does not hate the act of divorce, otherwise, He would not have given guidelines for obtaining a divorce. God hates sin which is the root cause of all divorce.

Conclusion

After analyzing these Old Testament passages there are a number of principles that are evident.

1. Not all divorces are sin, but the root cause of all divorce is sin.
2. God threatened to divorce Israel.
3. God commanded divorce in order to protect the Messianic line from contamination by pagan intermarriage.
4. God desires reconciliation for separated and divorced people.
5. God places strict demands on spiritual leaders—including a prohibition against marrying a divorced person.
6. God hates sin which is the root cause of all divorce.

Chapter Four

The Teachings of Jesus

The teachings of Jesus about divorce and remarriage are the focal point for the current interpretative controversies in the church. Everyone appeals to Christ's teaching as the substantive basis for their particular viewpoint. The teachings of Jesus are recorded in four separate passages in the Gospels. Although we will discuss each of these passages, the majority of our discussion will center in Matthew 19 since all the elements of Christ's teaching on the subject are found in that single passage. Before analyzing these verses I want you to read each of the sections dealing with divorce and remarriage.

> But I say unto you, That whosoever shall put away his wife, saving for the cause of fornication, causeth her to commit adultery: and whosoever shall marry her that is divorced committeth adultery.
>
> Matthew 5:32

> The Pharisees also came unto him, tempting him, and saying unto him, Is it lawful for a man to put away his wife for every cause?

And he answered and said unto them, Have ye not read, that he which made them at the beginning made them male and female,

And said, For this cause shall a man leave father and mother, and shall cleave to his wife: and they twain shall be one flesh?

Wherefore they are no more twain, but one flesh. What therefore God hath joined together, let not man put asunder.

They say unto him, Why did Moses then command to give a writing of divorcement, and to put her away?

He saith unto them, Moses because of the hardness of your hearts suffered you to put away your wives: but from the beginning it was not so.

And I say unto you, Whosover shall put away his wife, except it be for fornication, and shall marry another, committeth adultery: and whoso marrieth her which is put away doth commit adultery.

His disciples say unto him, If the case of the man be so with his wife, it is not good to marry.

But he said unto them, All men cannot receive this saying, save they to whom it is given.

For there are some eunuchs, which were so born from their mother's womb: and there are some eunuchs, which were made eunuchs of men: and there be eunuchs, which have made themselves eunuchs for the kingdom of heaven's sake. He that is able to receive it, let him receive it.

Matthew 19:3–12

And the Pharisees came to him, and asked him, Is it lawful for a man to put away his wife? tempting him.

And he answered and said unto them, What did Moses command you?

And they said, Moses suffered to write a bill of divorcement, and to put her away.

> And Jesus answered and said unto them, For the hardness of your heart he wrote you this precept.
>
> But from the beginning of the creation God made them male and female.
>
> For this cause shall a man leave his father and mother, and cleave to his wife;
>
> And they twain shall be one flesh: so then they are no more twain, but one flesh.
>
> What therefore God hath joined together, let not man put asunder.
>
> And in the house his disciples asked him again of the same matter.
>
> And he saith unto them, Whosoever shall put away his wife, and marry another, committeth adultery against her.
>
> And if a woman shall put away her husband, and be married to another, she committeth adultery.
>
> Mark 10:2–12

> Whosoever putteth away his wife, and marrieth another, committeth adultery: and whosoever marrieth her that is put away from her husband committeth adultery.
>
> Luke 16:18

Stop! Did you read these verses? If you did not—please go back and read them.

What Is the General Teaching of Jesus?

In Luke 16:18 we find the general teaching of Jesus that presents God's ideal: one man, one woman, for one lifetime. Jesus said, "Whosoever putteth away his wife, and marrieth another, committeth adultery: and whosoever marrieth her that is put away from her husband committeth adultery."

In this verse, as in Mark 10:11, 12, there are no exceptions that allow divorce. Jesus made a clear statement: If you divorce your wife and marry another, you have committed adultery.

Some use these verses to suggest that Jesus is teaching that there are no exceptions, no biblical grounds for divorce. But we cannot accept only those verses and ignore the other passages of Scripture where Jesus dealt with the issue. When we study the Scriptures, we must compare all passages on a particular subject, doctrine, or teaching. In Luke 16 and Mark 10, Jesus is giving the ideal. In Matthew 19 He gives the exception.

This is not unusual in Scripture. In Exodus 20 God says, "Thou shalt not kill." That is a clear-cut, absolute statement. But there were exceptions. For example, the Old Testament penalty for adultery was death. In Exodus, God gave the overall teaching: "Thou shalt not kill." In other passages He cited the exceptions. In Mark and Luke, Christ is giving the ideal standard for marriage, whereas in Matthew He is giving the exceptions to that standard.

Can a Woman Divorce Her Husband?

> And he saith unto them, Whosoever shall put away his wife, and marry another, committeth adultery against her.
>
> And if a woman shall put away her husband, and be married to another, she committeth adultery.
>
> Mark 10:11, 12

Mark 10:11, 12 teaches an interesting principle. *Divorce can originate with either partner.* The Old Testament teachings dealt specifically with the man who delivered the bill of divorcement to his wife. Could a woman divorce a man? Yes. In Mark 10:11 Jesus warns the man about divorcing his wife. Mark 10:12 warns the woman who divorces her husband.

Did Jesus Do Away With the Old Testament Teaching About Divorce and Remarriage?

The teaching of the Old Testament is clear in regard to divorce and remarriage. We identified several important biblical principles in Deuteronomy 24 that relate to the subject of divorce.

1. Divorce was man-made. God instituted marriage; He did not institute divorce. God instituted guidelines for controlling it. God commanded permanence in marriage; He conceded to grounds for divorce.
2. Divorce was permitted on the grounds of sexual misconduct that was less than adultery.
3. Divorce required a legal document, breaking the marriage covenant to the same degree that death breaks the marriage covenant.
4. Remarriage was permitted.
5. The divorced person was not allowed to return to the first husband after remarriage.
6. Divorce provided moral and financial protection to the woman.
7. God commands permanence in marriage. That is God's ideal. But in the context of Deuteronomy 24, He conceded to divorce. These principles can be reduced to three basic concepts. *God commands permanence in marriage. God permits divorce. God permits remarriage.* These fundamental concepts are clearly taught in the Pentateuch.

Whether you believe in divorce in the New Testament or not, you must conclude that in the Old Testament it was permitted along with remarriage. Those who believe that there are no biblical grounds for divorce and remarriage in the New Testament argue that Christ gave a new teaching on the subject that supercedes the Old Testament teaching.

Did Jesus close the door on the Old Testament divorce teaching and give a new set of principles regarding divorce? To answer that question we must examine Christ's teaching in Matthew 5:17–32. Read this passage carefully and note the underlined sections.

> Think not that I am come to destroy the law, or the prophets: I am not come to destroy, but to fulfil.
>
> For verily I say unto you, Till heaven and earth pass, one jot or one tittle shall in no wise pass from the law, till all be fulfilled.
>
> Whosoever therefore shall break one of these least commandments, and shall teach men so, he shall be called the least in the kingdom of heaven: but whosoever shall do and teach them, the same shall be called great in the kingdom of heaven.
>
> For I say unto you, That except your righteousness shall exceed the righteousness of the scribes and Pharisees, ye shall in no case enter into the kingdom of heaven.
>
> Ye have heard that it was said by them of old time, Thou shalt not kill; and whosoever shall kill shall be in danger of the judgment:
>
> But I say unto you, That whosoever is angry with his brother without a cause shall be in danger of the judgment: and whosoever shall say to his brother, Raca, shall be in danger of the council: but whosoever shall say, Thou fool, shall be in danger of hell fire.
>
> Therefore if thou bring thy gift to the altar, and there rememberest that thy brother hath aught against thee;
>
> Leave there thy gift before the altar, and go thy way; first be reconciled to thy brother, and then come and offer thy gift.

> Agree with thine adversary quickly whiles thou art in the way with him; lest at any time the adversary deliver thee to the judge, and the judge deliver thee to the officer, and thou be cast into prison.
>
> Verily I say unto thee, Thou shalt by no means come out thence, till thou hast paid the uttermost farthing.
>
> Ye have heard that it was said by them of old time, Thou shalt not commit adultery:
>
> But I say unto you, That whosoever looketh on a woman to lust after her hath committed adultery with her already in his heart.
>
> And if thy right eye offend thee, pluck it out, and cast it from thee: for it is profitable for thee that one of thy members should perish, and not that thy whole body should be cast into hell.
>
> And if thy right hand offend thee, cut it off, and cast it from thee: for it is profitable for thee that one of thy members should perish, and not that thy whole body should be cast into hell.
>
> It hath been said, Whosoever shall put away his wife, let him give her a writing of divorcement:
>
> But I say unto you, That whosoever shall put away his wife, saving for the cause of fornication, causeth her to commit adultery: and whosoever shall marry her that is divorced committeth adultery.
>
> Matthew 5:17–32 (emphasis added)

This section of the Sermon on the Mount begins with Jesus stating that He did not come to "destroy the law" but rather to "fulfil" it. The context of this passage clearly indicates that part of the Law which He had in mind was the law governing divorce and remarriage (vv. 31, 32). He did not come to destroy that Law! In this section the words, "It hath been said" and "I say unto you" occur six times. Jesus told the people that He had not come to do away with the Law, but to fulfill it. Notice in verse 21, He states, "Ye have heard that it was said by them of old time, Thou shalt not kill," and in verse 22 He counters, "But I say unto you, that whosoever is angry with his brother without a cause shall be in danger of judgment." Did His counterstatement imply that the commandment "Thou shalt not kill" was no longer relevant? No—He was showing the intent and purpose of that commandment. He was saying, "I want to remind you that the Old Testament says you shall not kill, but the underlying meaning is that you are not to hate your brother." Christ is not voiding the Old Testament Law, He is teaching the underlying intent of that Law.

In verse 27, Christ states, "Thou shalt not commit adultery" and in verse 27 He states, "But I say unto you, That whosoever looketh on a woman to lust after her hath committed adultery with her already in his heart." Jesus was not nullifying the Old Testament Law regarding adultery. Jesus was condemning the Pharisees who were proud that they had not committed the physical act of adultery but who were consumed with adulterous lust. Again, He is emphasizing the intent of the law.

In verses 31 and 32, Jesus is using this same pedagogical method. In verse 31 He gives the Old Testament Law, "Whosoever shall put away his wife, let him give her a writing of divorcement" and in verse 32 He continues, "But I say unto you, That whosoever shall put away his wife, saving for the cause of fornication, causeth her to commit adultery: and whosoever shall marry her that is divorced committeth adultery." Jesus is not nullifying the Old Testament Law of divorce any more than He nullified the Old Testament Law on murder and adultery. Rather, He was reminding them of the intent of the Law—to enhance the permanence and fidelity of marriage. He was emphasizing the lack of commitment to marriage. The Pharisees argued and debated over the specific technical grounds for divorce while ignoring a commitment to the permanence of marriage.

Let me give a simple illustration. Liberty University has a dress code that requires men to wear a shirt and tie to class. That is the law, but you ought to see the way some people conform to it. I have seen guys in T-shirts with a tie on, which technically meets the basic requirements of the law. I have seen plaid wool shirts and striped ties. That attire meets the letter of the law. But those outfits miss the intent and purpose of the law, which is to be neat and properly attired in clothing that looks pleasantly coordinated.

That is what the Pharisees were doing. They were too wrapped up with the legal details of the Law and missed out on the real issue of marriage. The quesion is not "What are the technical grounds for divorce?" The real question is "How can I keep the marriage together?"

What Is the Teaching in Matthew 19?

> The Pharisees also came unto him, tempting him, and saying unto him, Is it lawful for a man to put away his wife for every cause?
>
> And he answered and said unto them, Have ye not read, that he which made them at the beginning made them male and female,
>
> And said, For this cause shall a man leave father and mother, and shall cleave to his wife: and they twain shall be one flesh?
>
> Wherefore they are no more twain, but one flesh. What therefore God hath joined together, let not man put asunder.
>
> They say unto him, Why did Moses then command to give a writing of divorcement, and to put her away?
>
> He saith unto them, Moses because of the hardness of your hearts suffered you to put away your wives: but from the beginning it was not so.

> And I say unto you, Whososever shall put away his wife, except it be for fornication, and shall marry another, committeth adultery: and whoso marrieth her which is put away doth commit adultery.
>
> His disciples say unto him, If the case of the man be so with his wife, it is not good to marry.
>
> But he said unto them, All men cannot receive this saying, save they to whom it is given.
>
> For there are some eunuchs, which were so born from their mother's womb: and there are some eunuchs, which were made eunuchs of men: and there be eunuchs, which have made themselves eunuchs for the kingdom of heaven's sake. He that is able to receive it, let him receive it.
>
> Matthew 19:3–12

The focal Scripture on divorce and remarriage is found in Matthew 19. The Pharisees came to Jesus tempting Him and asking, "Is it lawful for a man to put away his wife for every cause?" The Jews were divided into two schools of thought on divorce. The school of Shammai believed that the only legal grounds for divorce was adultery. The school of Hillel believed that anything was grounds for divorce—a wife who talked too loudly or burned supper.

The Pharisees asked Jesus a very specific question: Is it lawful for a man to divorce his wife for *every cause?* Jesus was addressing the loose, liberal interpretation of the school of Hillel.

Christ answered by reminding the Pharisees of the commitment of marriage. He pointed out that God established marriage to bring two people together into one flesh: they were to become one person, one mind, one heart. God also intended for them to be secure. "What therefore God hath joined together, let not man put asunder." Jesus was saying, "You are arguing over the causes of divorce, but you have missed God's original plan and will for marriage."

In verses 7 and 8, the Pharisees brought up the concession of Moses, and Jesus answered that divorce was allowed because of the "hardness of your hearts."

Notice that divorce was not commanded by Moses. Divorce was "suffered." Moses permitted or tolerated divorce. He did not sanction and approve it. Many people claim to get a divorce because "the Lord told me to do it," but there is no biblical basis for that in any of the Scripture. Divorce is allowed, it is permitted, it is tolerated. It is not commanded.

Divorce was not God's original plan. The time line that began with Adam and Eve illustrates God's original plan for marriage. In the innocent state of the Garden of Eden, God gave His ultimate plan. There was no need for divorce laws because Adam and Eve were perfect. But sin entered into the human race—hardness of the heart. Through Moses God set up criteria for controlling divorce. When Jesus addressed this subject, He said, "I want to bypass all of the laws and remind you that God's ultimate plan and will is permanence in the marital relationship."

But Jesus recognized that we live in a sinful world. The problem in the Old Testament is the same problem we have in the twentieth century. Those who argue that Jesus wanted us to go back to the Garden of Eden and impose God's ideal on everyone in our society have forgotten that we are still living in a sinful world. When we take a stringent view on the subject of divorce and remarriage we fail to recognize the sinfulness of the society around us. We face the same problems today that Moses faced—the hardness of people's hearts.

What Grounds Did Jesus Give for Divorce?

Two crucial issues are addressed in verse 9: the basis for divorce and the basis of remarriage. Jesus said, "Whosoever shall put away his wife, except it be for fornication, and shall marry another, committeth adultery: and whoso marrieth her which is put away doth commit adultery." The key phrase is called the "exception clause"—"except it be for fornication." This phrase has been interpreted in three basic views:

The Engagement View. This view holds that the word *fornication*—the Greek word *porneia*—refers specifically to premarital sex. In New Testament times marriage actually began with the engagement covenant. When the engagement was made public, those people were legally married, though the marriage was not finalized until twelve to fifteen months later. The engagement theory suggests that the only grounds for divorce is unfaithfulness during the engagement period. After the couple is married, there are no biblical grounds for divorce, according to the engagement view.

This theory is difficult to accept because the word *porneia,* although it does refer in some passages to premarital sex, refers throughout Scripture to illicit sexual relationships in general. In this passage, Jesus is not dealing with engagement at all. He is discussing *marriage.* He also quotes from the Old Testament (Genesis 2 and Deuteronomy 24) and both of those passages deal with marriage, not engagement.

The Incest View. People who hold this view believe that the word *porneia* refers to the marrying of a close relative. In 1 Corinthians 5 *porneia* does obviously refer to an incestuous relationship. But if we accept this view, the whole argument is built on an exception rather than the rule. Second, the argument that divorce is only permissable in the case of incest is totally outside Leviticus 18:6–18, where the Old Testament Law dealt with the issue of incest. If Jesus really meant *porneia* to refer to incest, why did He not refer to the Old Testament Law prohibiting such marriages?

If Jesus is not talking about engagement and premarital sex or incest, what is He talking about? What is the third view? When is divorce permissable?

The Illicit Sex View. The third interpretation, the illicit sex theory, holds that *porneia* refers to illicit sexual intercourse in general. It is a broad term that can refer to all types of sexual immorality including incest, sodomy, harlotry, perversion, and all sexual sin before and after marriage. The word *porneia* comes from the verb *porneuo* which means to prostitute one's body or to give oneself to unlawful sexual intercourse.

Where else is this word used in Scripture? In 1 Corinthians 5:1 Paul defines *fornication* as an incestuous and adulterous relationship.

> It is reported commonly that there is fornication among you, and such fornication as is not so much as named among the Gentiles, that one should have his father's wife.
>
> 1 Corinthians 5:1

In this example *porneia* describes the sin of having a sexual relationship with a close relative.

Jude wrote in verse 7 of his book of the *porneia* of Sodom and Gomorrah.

> Even as Sodom and Gomorrah, and the cities around them in like manner, giving themselves over to fornication, and going after strange flesh, are set forth for an example, suffering the vengeance of eternal fire.
>
> Jude 7

In this case *porneia* refers to the sin of homosexuality. He describes it as "going after strange flesh."

Paul uses *porneia* in 1 Corinthians 7 to refer to premarital sex.

> Now concerning the things whereof ye wrote unto me: It is good for a man not to touch a woman.

> Nevertheless, to avoid fornication, let every man have his own wife, and let every woman have her own husband.
>
> 1 Corinthians 7:1, 2

Porneia is used throughout Scripture to refer to different types of sexual activity. So what did Jesus actually say in Matthew 19:9? "Whosoever shall put away his wife, except it be for fornication [*porneia*—adultery, homosexuality, incest, perversion, prostitution] and shall marry another, committeth adultery."

In contrast to the school of Hillel, which allowed divorce for any trivial reason, Jesus said that sexual immorality was the only allowance for divorce. This teaching of Jesus is in keeping with the Old Testament. God threatened Israel with divorce on the grounds of sexual immorality.

> They say, If a man put away his wife, and she go from him, and become another man's, shall he return to her again? shall not that land be greatly polluted? but thou hast played the harlot with many lovers; yet return again to me, saith the Lord.
>
> Jeremiah 3:1

Even in using divorce as an illustration of His spiritual relationship with Israel, the biblical grounds for securing that divorce is the same as outlined by Jesus—sexual immorality. In the context of Matthew 19 that sexual immorality could refer to adultery, homosexuality, incest, prostitution, or sexual perversion. These are biblically acceptable grounds for divorce as given by Jesus.

What About Remarriage?

Did Jesus permit remarriage after divorce? Those who hold to the engagement theory believe that because the marriage was never consummated, remarriage is permissable. Those who believe in the incest theory allow for divorce, but do not permit remarriage. Those who believe that *porneia* refers to illicit sex in general have two positions: (1)There may be biblical grounds for divorce, but remarriage is not permissable. (2)If there are biblical grounds for divorce, there is a biblical reason to remarry. The key to deciding between these two positions is found in understanding the context of Christ's teaching and the meaning of the exception clause.

In Luke 16:18 Jesus dealt with the adultery inherent in divorce and remarriage, and He mentioned the consequences of both. In Matthew 19:9 He allows for an exception, and the exception appears to be given for both divorce and remarriage. The two schools of interpretation prevalent in Jesus' day, the schools of Shammai and Hillel, both believed that a legitimate biblical divorce allowed remarriage. If Christ had intended to prohibit remarriage, He probably would have made it much clearer than He did in this passage. In both the Old Testament and the prevailing viewpoints in Christ's day, remarriage was always permitted based upon an appropriate bill of divorcement. Consequently, the people to whom Christ was giving this teaching on divorce presupposed the legitimacy of remarriage after proper grounds for divorce.

A proper understanding of the "exception clause" is necessary in order to determine whether or not a person can remarry after divorce.

> And I say unto you, Whosoever shall put away his wife, except it be for fornication, and shall marry another, committeth adultery: and whoso marrieth her which is put away doth commit adultery.
>
> Matthew 19:9

The issue here is actually simple to understand but difficult to solve. Does the exception clause refer only to divorce, or to remarriage as well? I believe the exception refers both to the act of divorce and the act of remarriage. If a person has a biblical divorce, that innocent person is free to remarry.

I believe rather than emphasizing the putting away of the wife or marrying another, Jesus emphasized committing adultery. Jesus was saying that divorce and remarriage not based on a biblical allowance was adulterous. If a divorce was granted on a biblical basis, *porneia,* then the innocent party had the opportunity to remarry. Remarriage was not required, but the party did not sin by remarrying. Paul gives further insight to the issue of remarriage in his writings, and we will discuss it in detail in the chapter dealing with the teaching of Paul.

Conclusion

As He usually did, Jesus encouraged God's ideal for marriage. While there are biblical grounds for divorce, divorce is *not* a right. I have met families who are falling apart and claim they have a right to divorce. No Christian has that right. We have every reason and opportunity to reconcile our problems, to come together, and stay together. Even though God permitted divorce, God's ultimate plan and will is for people to stay together.

But Jesus did recognize that we live in a sinful world. The ideal state seen in the Garden of Eden was ruined when sin entered the world. Because of the hardness of their hearts, God allowed Moses to instruct the Israelites on how to write a bill of divorcement. Jesus did not condone divorce, but He recognized that the world is sinful.

Jesus therefore permitted divorce on the basis of sexual sin and allowed remarriage to the innocent party after divorce. Does this position open up doors for divorce in the church? No. We ought to preach against divorce. We ought to urge reconciliation. We ought to encourage people to work out their problems and stay together.

Some people who do not believe in eternal security use a similar argument: "If we teach eternal security, then people will just get saved to go out and sin!" In reality, once a believer understands salvation and what God has done for him, he wants to live for Christ. When Christians understand God's plan for marriage, they will also understand what God wants them to do to preserve their marriage in a sinful world.

Chapter Five

Divorce and the Teaching of Paul

In previous chapters we established that the Old Testament gives three basic principles related to marriage and divorce: *God's ultimate priority is that marriage be a permanent relationship, a covenant broken only by the death of one of the partners; God permitted divorce and instituted guidelines for controlling it; God did allow those who had a legitimate biblical divorce to remarry.* We have also studied three principles regarding marriage and divorce from the teaching of Jesus: Jesus intended permanence in marriage; Jesus did make allowances for divorce on the basis of adultery or immorality; Jesus did allow remarriage if the divorce was biblical. The teaching of Jesus did not differ from the teaching of the Old Testament. What about the teaching of Paul? With the above principles in mind, we will examine two Pauline passages dealing with divorce and remarriage—Romans 7 and 1 Corinthians 7.

Is Death the Only Means of Breaking the Marriage Covenant?

Know ye not, brethren, (for I speak to them that know the law,) how that the law hath dominion over a man as long as he liveth?

For the woman which hath an husband is bound by the law to her husband so long as he liveth; but if the husband be dead, she is loosed from the law of her husband.

So then if, while her husband liveth, she be married to another man, she shall be called an adulteress: but if her husband be dead, she is free from that law; so that she is no adulteress, though she be married to another man.

Wherefore, my brethren, ye also are become dead to the law by the body of Christ; that ye should be married to another, even to him who is raised from the dead, that we should bring forth fruit unto God.

Romans 7:1–4

In Romans 7:2, we read: "For the woman which hath an husband is bound by the law to her husband so long as he liveth; but if the husband be dead, she is loosed from the law of her husband."

Those who advocate the position that there are no New Testament biblical grounds for divorce do so on the basis of this passage. Verse 3 seems to further uphold this position: "So then if, while her husband liveth, she be married to another man, she shall be called an adulteress: but if her husband be dead, she is free from that law; so that she is no adulteress, though she be married to another man." On the authority of these verses, some people write and teach that a divorced person who remarries is living in adultery. The passage clearly states that death releases the surviving partner, but remarriage before death constitutes adultery.

How can we deal with this passage in the light of Old Testament teaching and the teaching of Jesus? A prominent theologian, Archbishop Trench, said, "We are not to expect in every place the whole circle of Christian truth. . . . Nothing is proved by the absence of a doctrine from one passage which is clearly stated in others. . . . For all things are not taught in every place."

We must compare Scripture with Scripture. We saw this illustrated in the teaching of Jesus. In Matthew 5:19 Jesus gave the exception clause, the basis for legitimate divorce. In Luke and Mark, Christ did not give that exception clause. A study of only Mark and Luke leads to the logical conclusion that Jesus said there are no biblical grounds for divorce. But Mark and Luke record the general principle for marriage: one man, one woman, for one lifetime. In Matthew Jesus gives the exception.

We cannot read Romans 7 and ignore everything else the Bible says about divorce. We must compare it with 1 Corinthians 7, Matthew 5 and 19, Deuteronomy 24, and Genesis 2.

If Paul believed there were exceptions for divorce, why did he not mention them in Romans 7? Because his intended application of the passage made any exception clause unnecessary. Paul was using marriage as an illustration of a *theological truth.* He was not teaching on divorce or remarriage. He was trying to give an analogy of how we have died to the law through Christ and are now married to Christ. He was simply using marriage to illustrate his point.

Jesus also used illustrations. In Matthew 5:21, 22 we read, "Ye have heard that it was said by them of old time, Thou shalt not kill; and whosoever shall kill shall be in danger of the judgment: But I say unto you, That whosoever is angry with his brother without a cause shall be in danger of the judgment."

Jesus said, "Thou shalt not kill." If we take that one statement and isolate it from the rest of Scripture, we would have to conclude that Christians ought to totally and completely oppose capital punishment. If we did not regard the Scripture that tells us, "Whoso sheddeth man's blood, by man shall his blood be shed" (Genesis 9:16), we would have to struggle with the whole issue of war. Would it be right for a Christian to serve in the military? Is it right to go to war? Is it right to defend myself if in that defense I am compelled to kill another human being?

When a general principle is given in Scripture, the exceptions to that principle must be sought in the overall teaching of Scripture. ***We cannot take one verse and isolate it from the rest of Scripture.***

In Romans 7 Paul distinguishes between the Law in general and the law of marriage. To which law was Paul referring in verse 1? Some commentators suggest he referred to the civil law of his day, but I believe he was talking specifically about Mosaic Law. Within that Law were many regulations governing marriage: who could be married, when to be married, and rules of divorce and remarriage.

When Paul wrote about the law that governs marriage (verse 2), he did not include all the laws pertaining to marriage. He took one dimension of the law of marriage from the overall Mosaic Law and used it to illustrate a point.

Paul limited his illustration by choosing the specific law of marriage that fit his intended application in verse 4: "Wherefore, my brethren, ye also are become dead to the law by the body of Christ; that ye should be married to another, even to him who is raised from the dead, that we should bring forth fruit unto God."

Through the Body of Christ we have died to the Old Testament Law that we should be married to Jesus Christ to bring forth fruit unto God, the ultimate purpose of our holy marital relationship.

In these verses Paul deals only with the wife because he was illustrating the relationship between Christ and His church.

We are the bride of Christ, the wife. Paul limited his discussion to a specific law and to one part of that law, so the illustration fit its intended purpose—to illustrate the relationship we have with Jesus Christ.

Does Romans chapter 7 teach anything about marriage? Yes. It reemphasizes the permanence God wants in the marriage relationship. Does Romans 7 teach that death is the only thing that frees one from the marital relationship and that divorce and remarriage constitute adultery? Yes and no. Yes—in certain cases it is true. No—on the basis of a divorce granted on biblical grounds, it is not true.

Are There Any Grounds for Divorce Apart From Adultery?

> And unto the married I command, yet not I, but the Lord, Let not the wife depart from her husband:
>
> But and if she depart, let her remain unmarried, or be reconciled to her husband: and let not the husband put away his wife.
>
> But to the rest speak I, not the Lord: If any brother hath a wife that believeth not, and she be pleased to dwell with him, let him not put her away.
>
> And the woman which hath an husband that believeth not, and if he be pleased to dwell with her, let her not leave him.
>
> For the unbelieving husband is sanctified by the wife, and the unbelieving wife is sanctified by the husband: else were your children unclean; but now are they holy.
>
> But if the unbelieving depart, let him depart. A brother or a sister is not under bondage in such cases: but God hath called us to peace.
>
> For what knowest thou, O wife, whether thou shalt save thy husband? or how knowest thou, O man, whether thou shalt save thy wife?

> But as God hath distributed to every man, as the Lord hath called every one, so let him walk. And so ordain I in all churches.
>
> Is any man called being circumcised? let him not become uncircumcised. Is any called in uncircumcision? let him not be circumcised.
>
> Circumcision is nothing, and uncircumcision is nothing, but the keeping of the commandments of God.
>
> Let every man abide in the same calling wherein he was called.
>
> Art thou called being a servant? care not for it: but if thou mayest be made free, use it rather.
>
> For he that is called in the Lord, being a servant, is the Lord's freeman: likewise also he that is called, being free, is Christ's servant.
>
> Ye are bought with a price; be not ye the servants of men.
>
> Brethren, let every man, wherein he is called, therein abide with God.
>
> Now concerning virgins I have no commandment of the Lord: yet I give my judgment, as one that hath obtained mercy of the Lord to be faithful.
>
> I suppose therefore that this is good for the present distress, I say, that it is good for a man so to be.
>
> Art thou bound unto a wife? seek not to be loosed. Art thou loosed from a wife? seek not a wife.
>
> But and if thou marry, thou hast not sinned; and if a virgin marry, she hath not sinned. Nevertheless such shall have trouble in the flesh: but I spare you.
>
> 1 Corinthians 7:10–28

Paul wrote about divorce in 1 Corinthians 7:10, 11. "And unto the married I command, yet not I, but the Lord. Let not the wife depart from her husband: But and if she depart, let her remain unmarried, or be reconciled to her husband: and let not the husband put away his wife."

The word *depart* in verse 10 is the word *chorizo,* which means to "divide, separate, or put asunder." In secular Greek writing it is a technical term used for divorce. The same word was used in Matthew 19 when Christ said, "What therefore God hath joined together, let no man put asunder." Clearly, Paul is writing about divorce—not merely living apart or legal separation—in 1 Corinthians 7.

The expression "put away" at the end of verse 11 comes from the Greek *aphiemi,* meaning to "let go or send away." It can also be used in a business context to mean the cancellation of a debt. In the Lord's Prayer it is translated, "Forgive us our debts." Paul used the same idea when he told the Corinthians, "Don't put away your wife. Don't cancel that relationship."

Paul taught permanence in the marriage relationship, and he went a step further. Even after a legal divorce, Paul urged everything possible be done to achieve a reconciliation. If we really live for God, there is no reason for divorce. If separation should come, reconciliation is God's ultimate desire.

Does separation from a spouse imply the freedom to date other people? What about the need for friendship or help with the unbearable loneliness? Dating cultivates relationships that may detract from the possibility of reconciliation. A separated person may think there is no hope for the marriage, but as long as he is seeking God's will, there is hope. God can solve the problem. The worst thing a separated person can do is begin dating. Too many times, couples date during a separation and marry after a divorce decree, then months later the first husband finally gets saved or the wife decides to serve God. The divorced couple could have been reconciled, but now it is impossible. *Through prayer, counseling, and forgiveness, everything possible should be done during that period of separation to seek reconciliation.*

What About the Saved/Unsaved Spouse?

In 1 Corinthians 7:12 Paul discusses the relationship between saved and unsaved spouses: "But to the rest speak I, not the Lord: If any brother hath a wife that believeth not, and she be pleased to dwell with him, let him not put her away. And the woman which hath an husband that believeth not, and if he be pleased to dwell with her, let her not leave him."

Paul did not mean that his admonition was less authoritative than that of Jesus. He wanted to say, "Christ did not address this particular situation. I am going to do it." Of course we believe he did so under the inspiration of the Holy Spirit and therefore his advice is binding.

Paul said that the unbelieving husband is sanctified by the wife and vice versa. This does not mean that the unbelieving spouse is saved because of the believer's faith, but that there is a witness to the love of Christ in the home. It is similar to the Old Testament concept of the covenant through which a circumcised boy became part of the covenant people. This did not guarantee his salvation based upon faith in the Messiah, but it did make the child part of the covenant people of God and opened to him all the advantages of a spiritual relationship where he could learn the Word of God.

So it is in marriage. Through the life, testimony, and witness of the saved partner, spiritual advantages are brought to the unsaved partner and the entire family. "Your children were unclean; but now they are holy." This does not mean that they are saved, but that they will have the advantage of a spiritual godly parent who can influence them for the sake of Christ.

Apparently the church at Corinth was dealing with a serious problem regarding an unsaved husband and wife, when one of the partners accepted Christ and a problem was created in the marriage. In 1 Corinthians 7:12–17 Paul addressed the situation by beginning: "But to the rest speak I, not the Lord."

Since we believe that all Scripture is God-breathed and inerrant, this passage is just as authoritative as the words Jesus spoke. Paul was saying, "I am going to give you an instruction concerning something Jesus did not deal with."

Paul then admonished the couple with one saved spouse to stay together if at all possible. Apparently, in the midst of pagan worship at Corinth, a husband or wife had been saved, and the unsaved partner continued in the pagan, idolatrous worship. The saved spouse was torn between loyalties to Christ and to the unsaved spouse. Paul's answer: Do all you can to stay together.

Paul gives three reasons for the couple to stay together: "For the unbelieving husband is sanctified by the wife, and the unbelieving wife is sanctified by the husband: else were your children unclean; but now are they holy."

Paul was not saying that the unsaved people were sanctified in the sense that they were automatically saved, but that through the example of the saved family member, a godly influence was exerted on that home. Paul reminded the Corinthians: "God hath called us to peace." One of the most devastating calamities in a family is divorce. Feelings of loneliness, guilt, and inferiority often result. Children of divorce suffer disastrous consequences. They want to love both parents. Deep emotional, psychological, and spiritual problems are frequently found in a broken home. Paul wrote to say, "You ought to stay together for the sake of your family, because divorce can bring only disruption and hurt to all of the people involved."

Paul wanted the mixed marriages to stay together, not only for the sake of the family and for the sake of peace, but also for the sake of personal testimony. In verse 16 he wrote: "For what knowest thou, O wife, whether thou shalt save thy husband? Or how knowest thou, O man, whether thou shalt save thy wife?"

Paul was not implying that the wife or husband had the capability of saving the unsaved spouse; only God through the finished work of Jesus Christ can save a soul. But Paul was saying that a personal testimony could win the unsaved partner to Christ. Paul was urging, "Make it your ultimate prayer and goal and objective to win that unsaved partner to Christ."

In verse 15 we find the heart of the controversy that surrounds 1 Corinthians 7. Paul writes, "But if the unbelieving depart, let him depart. A brother or a sister is not under bondage in such cases."

Notice that the action of departing was undertaken by the unbeliever, not the believer. There are two interpretations of the remainder of verse 15. The first holds that Paul was talking about a separation, not divorce. Those who take this position argue that if the unsaved person departs because of the faith of the believer, it is permissible to live separate one from another.

The other interpretation is that Paul is giving further biblical grounds for divorce. If the unbeliever divorces a husband or wife because of his or her faith in Jesus Christ, that divorce is legitimate and biblical. The saved person is not under obligation to the marriage covenant and is therefore free to remarry.

How can we choose between the two views? The word for "depart" is the Greek verb *chorizo,* a technical term for divorce. It is used in Matthew 19:6, "What therefore God hath joined together, let not man put asunder." The entire passage here clearly refers to divorce, not separation, and the word for "put asunder" is the same Greek verb *chorizo.* On this basis, I believe Paul was definitely referring to divorce, not separation.

Was the saved partner who had been divorced free to remarry? Paul wrote that a brother or sister was not under bondage. The term for bondage, from the Greek *douleo,* meant to "make someone a slave." If a slave was declared "not under bondage" in the legal documents of that day, his former owner had no claim on him and all legal obligations were broken. This same idea applies in the case of divorce in the situation of 1 Corinthians 7. The legal contract (the marriage covenant), was dissolved, and the innocent person was not under any obligation.

Paul used the same idea in 1 Corinthians 7:39. "The wife is bound by the law as long as her husband liveth; but if her husband be dead, she is at liberty to be married to whom she will; only in the Lord."

Paul was saying that the wife was bound by the law to her husband, but when he died she was no longer bound. The marriage covenant could be broken by death (v. 39) or by divorce (v. 15).

On the basis of the language of this passage and the general teaching of 1 Corinthians 7, I believe Paul added to the teaching of Jesus by saying that in one special circumstance—when an unbeliever divorced a believer on the basis of faith in Christ—a biblical divorce could be granted, and the saved person, no longer bound by the marriage, was free to marry. Are there grounds for divorce apart from adultery? Yes—when an unbeliever divorces a believer on the basis of the believer's faith in Christ.

What About Remarriage After a Divorce?

> Brethren, let every man, wherein he is called, therein abide with God.
>
> Now concerning virgins I have no commandment of the Lord: yet I give my judgment, as one that hath obtained mercy of the Lord to be faithful.
>
> I suppose therefore that this is good for the present distress, I say, that it is good for a man so to be.
>
> Art thou bound unto a wife? seek not to be loosed. Art thou loosed from a wife? seek not a wife.
>
> But and if thou marry, thou hast not sinned; and if a virgin marry, she hath not sinned. Nevertheless such shall have trouble in the flesh: but I spare you.
>
> 1 Corinthians 7:24–28

In verses 25 and 26 Paul addressed nonmarried people, virgins. He advised them to remain single because of the pressure of the age and the necessity of serving Christ and preaching the Gospel. Later he says, "I think you can care for the things of the Lord in a greater way than a married person. Your time and effort and talents can be maximized if you are single."

To the already married, Paul urged, "Seek not to be loosed." Because there are only two ways to be loosed from a wife—death and divorce—Paul was referring to divorce. No rational person would seek release from a marriage by desiring the death of his partner. He then asked, "Art thou loosed from a wife? Seek not a wife. But and if thou marry, thou hast not sinned; and if a virgin marry, she hath not sinned" (v. 28).

Who is being married in this verse? There are only three options. Paul could be talking to someone who has been divorced, a widow or a widower, or a virgin. I do not believe Paul was talking to virgins, because in the next clause he addresses virgins directly. So Paul is talking to people who have lost their mates through death or divorce. He told them, "But and if thou marry, thou hast not sinned." Paul said that if a person has been loosed through divorce, it is better not to marry, but if you do remarry, you have not sinned. But he adds a footnote in verse 28: "Nevertheless such shall have trouble in the flesh."

Paul wanted divorced people who remarried to know of the great likelihood that trouble waited ahead. Anyone who has studied secular or sacred writings, or articles or books on the subject of divorce and remarriage, can certainly determine that those who remarry after divorce are more likely to have trouble in the second marriage. Why? Because almost invariably, the same problems that brought about the deterioration of the first marriage will bring trouble to the second marriage if they are not resolved.

Paul ends the discussion by reminding the Corinthians of the Christian's commitment to marriage (1 Corinthians 7:39). Even though the Old Testament and Jesus and Paul give biblical grounds for divorce, both the Old and New Testaments, Moses, Jesus, and Paul all appealed for the same thing—permanence in marriage. When a Christian enters a marriage and stands at the altar, he is making a lifelong commitment to that relationship. We are not to enter marriage with the idea that if it does not work, divorce is always an option. Though there are biblical grounds for divorce, Christians have less reason to seek a divorce than anyone, because we have the Word of God as our guideline and the Holy Spirit living within us. We have all the spiritual advantages to bring unity to the marriage relationship, so a Christian's divorce is the ultimate demonstration of failure within a marriage. There may be problems on both sides of any marriage, but as Christians we ought to do all we can to help people stay together, not pull them apart.

Conclusion

What does Paul teach concerning divorce and remarriage? There are four major conclusions that can be identified in Paul's writings.

1. *He advocates permanence in the marriage relationship* (1 Corinthians 7:39, 40; Romans, 7:1–4).
2. *He advocates the reconciliation of divorced and separated parties* (1 Corinthians 7:10, 11).
3. *He permits divorce on the grounds of religious differences* (1 Corinthians 7:15).
4. *He permits remarriage after a legitimate divorce* (1 Corinthians 7:28).

Chapter Six

Divorce and the Church

In the last chapter we discussed Paul's teaching on the subject of divorce and remarriage. Paul advocates permanence in the marriage relationship and the reconciliation of separated and divorced parties. Paul also permits divorce on the grounds of religious differences and permits remarriage after a legitimate divorce. Given the fact that the Bible permits divorce and remarriage, how should the church relate to divorced and remarried members? Are they second-class citizens? Can they serve in the leadership of the church? If God has forgiven them, why can't their church?

Can a Divorced Person Be a Pastor or a Deacon?

One of the most frequently asked questions concerning divorce is whether or not a divorced person can be a pastor or a deacon. The church is divided over this issue with some people excluding divorcees from church leadership and others accepting them as both pastors and deacons. What does the Bible teach? Paul lists seventeen qualifications for pastors in 1 Timothy 3:1–7.

1. Blameless (above reproach)
2. Husband of one wife
3. Vigilant (temperate)
4. Sober (serious-minded)
5. Good behavior (orderly)
6. Given to hospitality
7. Apt to teach (skillful in teaching)
8. Not given to wine
9. No striker (physical violence)
10. Not greedy of filthy lucre
11. Patient
12. Not a brawler (quarrelsome)
13. Not covetous
14. Ruleth well his own house
15. Children in subjection
16. Not a novice (new convert)
17. Good report

It is clear from these requirements that God places stringent demands upon those who aspire to the office of pastor. The church has a clear responsibility toward those spiritual leaders. We are to care for them (1 Corinthians 9:1, 3–9), respect them (1 Thessalonians 5:12, 13), imitate them (Hebrews 13:7) and obey them (v. 17).

In looking at these qualifications, it appears that they can be reduced to two major categories. First, the pastor must be "blameless." The word utilized means "not able to be taken hold of, beyond reproach." The idea is that there should be nothing in the pastor's life or family that would bring reproach to the cause of Christ. The second major concept is "apt to teach" or skillful in teaching. It seems to me that the other fifteen qualifications fall under these categories with most of them relating to personal testimony.

How does all of this relate to a divorced person? The phrase that is utilized to bring divorce into the qualifications for a pastor is the one which states that a pastor must be "the husband of one wife." Notice in verse 12 that this is also a requirement for deacons. A pastor or a deacon is to be a "one-woman husband." What does Paul mean? There are a number of interpretations.

Some people believe *this excludes married men.* For instance, Roman Catholic dogma states that the "one woman" for a pastor is the church. Therefore, they believe all bishops and pastors within the church ought to be married to the church. First Timothy 4:3 reveals that one characteristic of false teachers is that they prohibit marriage. Furthermore, Paul says that a pastor should have his children in subjection, and it is difficult to have children if you are celibate!

The second interpretation *excludes single people.* Some believe Paul intended that pastors and deacons be married. This line of reasoning leads to the conclusion that pastors must also have more than one child. But this position contradicts 1 Corinthians 7:7, where Paul advocated that a single person could serve God better than a married person.

The third position holds that *this refers to the exclusion of polygamists*—pastors and deacons should not have more than one wife at a time. But polygamy was prohibited by Roman law, and neither the Greeks nor the Romans of the New Testament practiced polygamy. It would seem unnecessary that Paul would add this requirement if polygamy was already against the law.

The fourth position is that Paul *was excluding those who have been divorced, or those who have been divorced and remarried, from the office of pastor and deacon.* This is predicated upon the idea that God always demands greater requirements and qualifications of those in leadership.

In Leviticus 21 God legislated matters of holiness in priestly conduct and duties. A man had to meet certain requirements to be a priest. Notice the guidelines in verse 7. "They shall not take a wife that is a whore, or profane; neither shall they take a woman put away from her husband: for he is holy unto his God." The Old Testament prohibited priests from marrying women who had been divorced. Notice the disqualifications for priestly office: "For whatsoever man he be that hath a blemish . . . a blind man, or a lame, or he that hath a flat nose, or anything superfluous, or a man that is brokenfooted, or brokenhanded, or crookbackt, or a dwarf . . ." (vv. 18–20). Obviously God places greater demands on people in leadership roles.

God is teaching the same principle in 1 Timothy 3, placing greater demands and requirements upon those who assume spiritual leadership in the church—pastors and deacons. These are not suggestions, but qualifications to be found in the lives of men who feel called to leadership in the church.

It seems to me that the phrase "husband of one wife" excludes those who have been divorced, or divorced and remarried, from assuming the pastorate or becoming a deacon in the church. In verse 4 Paul adds that the pastor must rule his own house well and have his children in subjection. The word *rule* means to manage. The pastor and the deacon must manage their own houses well. Divorce is the ultimate act of mismanagement in one's household. Although there are legitimate grounds for divorce and people can be free to remarry, divorce is always the result of sin. Therefore, one who mismanaged the affairs of his own house does not qualify scripturally for a leadership position in the church.

Can a man who was divorced and remarried before he was saved hold the office of pastor or deacon? Even if the divorce took place before the man was saved, it appears that he is still excluded from these offices of leadership. Again, the standard of "blamelessness" in the community must be applied. However, I want to be careful at this point and not be too dogmatic. In my opinion, the qualifications still apply but you must decide that on your own before God and His Word.

Some believe that 2 Corinthians 5:17 promises that since "all things are become new," a previously divorced man could become a pastor. Although certainly our sins are forgiven when we are saved, the consequences of some sins have ongoing results in our lives. For example, if someone is heavily involved with drugs before he is saved, his burned-out brain is not replaced when he becomes a new creature in Christ. Even though the divorce occurred prior to salvation, it is likely that there will be ongoing problems with the former spouse and children that could negatively impact one's position of leadership.

Someone asked me, "Do you mean that a homosexual, a child molester, a rapist, or a murderer can be saved and become a pastor, but because I'm divorced God cannot use me?" The Bible is clear that a man must first prove himself and then rise to the office of pastor or deacon. We know that through the forgiveness of God a man can rise to leadership, but it must be clear in the minds of those who ordain him that all his problems are past, forgotten, forgiven, and reconciled. I think some sins would exclude a person from that ultimate position of leadership, just as certain body defects excluded priests from serving in the tabernacle and temple. Just because God has forgiven does not necessarily mean that person should assume a position of leadership.

What then can divorced people do in the church? Can they teach a Sunday-school class? Can they sing in the choir? Can they be evangelists? A divorced person can do all of those things, providing God has called him to those particular tasks. This limitation in 1 Timothy 3 is specifically for pastors and deacons. Many people who have been divorced and remarried, and have sought the forgiveness of God, have been mightily used of God in their church—apart from the offices of pastor and deacon.

Have you used a Scofield Bible, probably the most widely read Bible in the twentieth century? C. I. Scofield was divorced and remarried, but God used him in a wonderful way to influence the lives of thousands of people. Divorced people can and ought to serve in the church.

Suppose someone has been involved in permarital sexual relationships and later is married. Is that person in violation of the "one-woman husband" qualification because he has had a sexual relationship with someone other than his wife prior to marriage? Does that exclude anyone who has had premarital sex from becoming a pastor or deacon? No. I believe the Scriptures are clear that the sexual act does not constitute a marriage.

Whenever I counsel young people who have made that terrible moral mistake, I often find that someone has told them, "Because you have had a relationship with that person, in God's eyes you are married to that person." That is not biblically true. I always tell young people, "It may be the will of God for you to go ahead and get married, but you have made one mistake—don't make another by marrying the wrong person. Seek guidance and the advice of your parents and come together with a corporate decision that is indeed the will of God."

What If a Pastor or Deacon Commits Adultery?

Although premarital sex does not exclude a person from rising to leadership within the church, what about extramarital sex? What should happen when a pastor or a deacon has an adulterous relationship with someone? Does that act or that relationship exclude that person from ever becoming a pastor or a deacon for the rest of his life? Even though his marriage may stay together and the sin falls under the forgiveness of God, is the adulterous man excluded from leadership in the church?

There are two extreme approaches to this question. The first approach is, "Well, my pastor committed adultery, but since God has forgiven him, we forgive him. He can stay on as our pastor." The other extreme is, "Our pastor committed adultery, he made a mistake, he sinned against God. Let's beat him down for the rest of his life, so he will never do anything for God again."

The latter approach is taken too often. The biblical approach is somewhere between these two. When someone in the position of leadership violates moral integrity, he forfeits the position of leadership—because he must be blameless. We must then turn around and ask, "How can we lead you to repentence? How can we assist you toward restoration? How can we help?" According to the Word of God, we have an obligation to discipline. Church discipline necessitates the forfeiture of leadership, but at the same time we must love, forgive, and restore that person so that after a period of time, he can prove himself and his integrity again. We should help him find a different area where he can continue serving the Lord. I will deal with this issue in greater detail in chapter 7.

Can a widower remarry? Suppose a pastor's wife dies, and he remarries. Technically he is not a "one-woman husband," but I believe he is perfectly legitimate as a leader in the church because the underlying principle here is integrity of life-style and character.

What if a man feels the Lord has called him to be a pastor, but his wife has been previously divorced? Technically he meets the biblical requirements, but his wife does not. I personally believe that we are wise to reserve the position of blameless leadership for men who have not been divorced and whose wives have not been divorced. There is no clear statement in the New Testament about this situation, but because of the principles of Leviticus 21, I feel that God wants His leadership to be above reproach or question.

What About the Forgiveness of God?

> Therefore if any man be in Christ, he is a new creature: old things are passed away; behold, all things are become new.
>
> 2 Corinthians 5:17

If a person is divorced prior to salvation, can he become a pastor or deacon? We discussed this question briefly in the previous section of this chapter. There is a strong biblical case for the forgiveness of God—even in the case of a divorced person.

> He hath not dealt with us after our sins; nor rewarded us according to our iniquities.
>
> For as the heaven is high above the earth, so great is his mercy toward them that fear him.
>
> As far as the east is from the west, so far hath he removed our transgressions from us.
>
> Psalms 103:10–12

> In whom also ye are circumcised with the circumcision made without hands, in putting off the body of the sins of the flesh by the circumcision of Christ:
>
> Buried with him in baptism, wherein also ye are risen with him through the faith of the operation of God, who hath raised him from the dead.
>
> And you, being dead in your sins and the uncircumcision of your flesh, hath he quickened together with him, having forgiven you all trespasses;
>
> Colossians 2:11–13

> In whom we have redemption through his blood, the forgiveness of sins, according to the riches of his grace;
>
> Ephesians 1:7

At the moment of salvation we are new creatures in Christ. God has forgiven *all* our sins and *all things* are become new. Does this then mean that a person who is divorced ought to be accepted by the church as if he had never been divorced? If God has forgiven him and accepted him, then why won't the church? These are important questions which have no easy answers. First, *the person ought to be accepted as a first-class citizen in the church.* After all, the entire church is nothing more than a bunch of sinners saved by grace! Can the divorced person then become a pastor or a deacon? This is a substantially different question than whether or not he should be accepted in the church. We are talking about leadership—not citizenship. God has definite qualifications for leaders that are more stringent than what is required of the citizenship of His Kingdom. Certain people are excluded from the offices of pastor and deacon—brawlers, greedy, covetous, and so forth. Consequently, to hold a position that divorced people should not serve as pastor and deacon, based on 1 Timothy 3:2, is not discriminating against them or reducing them to second-class citizenship. It is a matter of accepting the biblical criteria for such leadership.

How Should the Church React to Separated and Divorced People?

What should the local church do with divorced people? First and foremost, the church should stress reconciliation. We ought to preach the ideal of marriage and give people the basic principles for success in their marital and family relationships. When marriages begin to fall apart, we ought to be instrumental in helping couples achieve a reconciliation. The church is the place where we can pray, teach, and guide people through the difficulties of marriage.

Next, the church ought to have an attitude of restoration. We are to meet people at their deepest point of need and restore them. People going through a divorce are experiencing extreme emotional and spiritual problems. A great sense of guilt, failure, loneliness, and the devastation of their self-image overwhelms them. Divorced people often feel more at home in a singles' bar than in a church! We ought to be committed to loving, forgiving, accepting, and rebuilding them.

B. R. Lakin, a friend and prominent evangelist, who is now in heaven, used to tell us how to respond to divorced people: "Be quick to forgive, slow to judge." But suppose the guilty party in a divorce remarries another. Are they living in a constant state of adultery?

There is no constant state of adultery. To say that it is constant would make divorce the unpardonable sin, which it is not. Someone who willfully violates Scripture to divorce and remarry can seek the forgiveness of God and be restored into fellowship in the church.

Suppose a Christian wants to divorce his wife on illegitimate grounds. What should the church do? First, we must exercise church discipline. We should go to that individual personally, plurally, and publicly, to do all we can to hinder the divorce. Jesus and Paul give us the strategy for doing this.

> Moreover if thy brother shall trespass against thee, go and tell him his fault between thee and him alone: if he shall hear thee, thou hast gained thy brother.
>
> But if he will not hear thee, then take with thee one or two more, that in the mouth of two or three witnesses every word may be established.
>
> And if he shall neglect to hear them, tell it unto the church: but if he neglect to hear the church, let him be unto thee as an heathen man and a publican.
>
> Matthew 18:15–17

> Brethren, if a man be overtaken in a fault, ye which are spiritual, restore such an one in the spirit of meekness; considering thyself, lest thou also be tempted.
>
> Galatians 6:1

If he proceeds with his plan, we must exercise discipline by putting him out of the church while praying that he will seek God's forgiveness. If he does repent, we should reconcile him into the fellowship of the church, even if he has remarried. Once he has the forgiveness of God and has genuinely repented, we ought to restore him, reconcile him, and eventually find him a place of service for the Lord.

What About Physical Abuse?

What about wife abuse? Does a person who has been physically abused have the right to divorce and remarry? This problem is increasing in our society, and church families are not immune to it. Some people suggest that because a woman should be in submission to her husband, she is obligated to stay with him no matter what the situation. That is ludicrous advice. If a woman is being physically abused and the welfare and emotional well-being of the children are in jeopardy, she ought to separate from her husband. She should find help from family or friends at a home for battered women or within the church. While this is not the basis for a biblical divorce, a battered woman has every right to separate from her husband for her own protection and for the protection of the children.

Conclusion

The church must never drop the banner of marital permanence. We should always preach that God's intention is one woman, one man, for a lifetime. We also must resist judging and discarding those who have gone through marital problems, divorce, and remarriage. We must love and accept them. We must be quick to forgive and slow to judge. Our church should be filled to capacity with sinners saved by grace, who can reach out and meet others at their point of need.

Chapter Seven

The Bible, Human Sexuality, and Adultery

We live in a sexually liberated society; the message of movies, magazines, novels and television is one of sexual freedom. The tragedy of the amoral culture is that it has infiltrated the church of Jesus Christ. Almost every week we hear of another pastor, missionary, or evangelist who has shipwrecked on the rocks of immorality—not to mention the lay people about whom we hear very little. Families have been torn apart, lives ruined, and ministries destroyed for a few moments of self-indulgent gratification. If ever there was a time to raise the standard of righteousness and promote and defend marital fidelity, it is now. We must understand the biblical criteria that relate to the whole area of human sexuality. Since adultery is one of the legitimate grounds for divorce, we need to examine this problem from a biblical perspective.

What Is the Purpose of Sex?

Sex is a gift from God. The Bible indicates a threefold purpose for the sexual relationship within marriage.

1. Procreation

> So God created man in his own image, in the image of God created he him; male and female created he them.
>
> And God blessed them, and God said unto them, Be fruitful, and multiply, and replenish the earth and subdue it: and have dominion over the fish of the sea, and over the fowl of the air, and over every living thing that moveth upon the earth.
>
> Genesis 1:27, 28

2. Unity

> Therefore shall man leave his father and his mother, and shall cleave unto his wife: and they shall be one flesh.
>
> And they were both naked, the man and his wife, and were not ashamed.
>
> 2:24, 25

In chapter 1, we dealt extensively with these verses and identified four specific principles that relate to the function of marriage.

1. Separation
2. Singleness
3. Synthesis
4. Shamelessness

The phrase that relates to the matter of human sexuality is that the two shall "become one flesh." This is both a sexual and personal union, the coming together of two people. This means that sex is more than a physical act—it is the merging together of two persons. It involves mind, body, and soul. There is no such thing as casual sex for physical gratification.

3. *Pleasure*

> Drink waters out of thine own cistern, and running waters out of thine own well.
>
> Let thy fountains be dispersed abroad, and rivers of waters in the streets.
>
> Let them be only thine own, and not strangers' with thee.
>
> Let thy fountain be blessed: and rejoice with the wife of thy youth.
>
> Let her be as the loving hind and pleasant roe; let her breasts satisfy thee at all times; and be thou ravished always with her love.
>
> Proverbs 5:15–19

> My beloved is white and ruddy, the chiefest among ten thousand.
>
> His head is as the most fine gold, his locks are bushy, and black as a raven.
>
> His eyes are as the eyes of doves by the rivers of waters, washed with milk, and fitly set.
>
> His cheeks are as a bed of spices, as sweet flowers: his lips like lilies, dropping sweet smelling myrrh.
>
> His hands are as gold rings set with the beryl: his belly is as bright ivory overlaid with sapphires.
>
> His legs are as pillars of marble, set upon sockets of fine gold: his countenance is as Lebanon, excellent as the cedars.

> His mouth is most sweet: yea, he is altogether lovely. This is my beloved, and this is my friend, O daughters of Jerusalem.
>
> Song of Solomon 5:10–16

> How beautiful are thy feet with shoes, O prince's daughter! the joints of thy thighs are like jewels, the work of the hands of a cunning workman.
>
> Thy navel is like a round goblet, which wanteth not liquor: thy belly is like an heap of wheat set about with lilies.
>
> Thy two breasts are like two young roes that are twins.
>
> Thy neck is as a tower of ivory; thine eyes like the fishpools in Heshbon, by the gate of Bath-rabbim: thy nose is as the tower of Lebanon which looketh toward Damascus.
>
> Thine head upon thee is like Carmel, and the hair of thine head like purple; the king is held in the galleries.
>
> How fair and how pleasant art thou, O love, for delights!
>
> This thy stature is like to a palm tree, and thy breasts to clusters of grapes.
>
> I said, I will go up to the palm tree, I will take hold of the boughs thereof: now also thy breasts shall be as clusters of the vine, and the smell of thy nose like apples;
>
> And the roof of thy mouth like the best wine for my beloved, that goeth down sweetly, causing the lips of those that are asleep to speak.
>
> I am my beloved's, and his desire is toward me.
>
> 7:1–10

These verses indicate that sex involves more than the conjugal act, it is the mutual enjoyment of one another's physical bodies. These verses also indicate that the act of sex is something to be enjoyed by mankind not endured. In fact, the "foreplay" indicated in these passages may relate to the "uncleanness" mentioned in Deuteronomy 24 (*see* chapter 2).

From these verses related to the subject of human sexuality there are a number of important biblical principles that merit attention.

1. *The gift of sex is to be exercised within the confinement of the commitment of marriage.* Extramarital and premarital sex are taboo for Christians.

2. *Sex is more than a physical act.* It is the merging together of two persons in mind, body, and soul. That is why there are such serious emotional and spiritual consequences when one violates God's principles.

3. *Sex is something that God intended for our enjoyment, not our endurance.*

4. *Human sexuality involves all of the activities that surround the conjugal act including the mutual enjoyment of one another's bodies.* Oftentimes I have people who state, "Well, I didn't go all the way." They utilize this kind of rationale to excuse the intense physical relationship that they had, assuming that they had not violated the Bible since they didn't actually commit the conjugal act. It is clear from the Song of Solomon that the act of sex includes the various activities that lead up to the actual conjugal act.

Why Is Adultery So Wrong?

Since we are bombarded with the message of the acceptability of sexual freedom from the culture-at-large, there is a tendency to minimize the serious nature of that sin. True, all sin is serious, and God's forgiveness is greater than any sin, but Scripture clearly teaches that adultery is grievous to the heart of God.

1. Adultery is a sin against God.

When Potiphar's wife attempted to seduce Joseph, he responded, "How then can I do this great wickedness, and sin against God?" (Genesis 39:9). Adultery is a violation of God's moral law.

> Thou shalt not commit adultery.
>
> Exodus 20:14

2. Adultery is a sin against the Holy Spirit.

Paul categorizes adultery as a sin different from all others. When anyone commits adultery, he is sinning against the Holy Spirit who indwells his body.

> What? know ye not that he which is joined to an harlot is one body? for two, saith he, shall be one flesh.
>
> But he that is joined unto the Lord is one spirit.
>
> Flee fornication. Every sin that a man doeth is without the body; but he that committeth fornication sinneth against his own body.
>
> What? know ye not that your body is the temple of the Holy Ghost which is in you, which ye have of God, and ye are not your own?
>
> For ye are bought with a price: therefore glorify God in your body, and in your spirit, which are God's.
>
> 1 Corinthians 6:16–20

3. Adultery is a sin against the Body of Christ.

As Christians we are members of the Body of Christ. Paul states, "Know ye not that your bodies are the members of Christ? shall I then take the members of Christ, and make them the members of an harlot? God forbid" (1 Corinthians

6:15). When one commits adultery, he not only sins against God and the Holy Spirit, he sins against the entire Body of Christ.

4. ***Adultery is a sin against one's partner.***

Marriage is a solemn covenant between husband and wife. This covenant includes fidelity to one another. When one partner commits adultery, he has sinned against the other partner and violated the covenant he made with God and his spouse. The trust that was violated may never be restored, even though God forgives and the marriage is rebuilt.

What Are the Consequences of Adultery?

In the Mosaic Law the penalty for adultery was death. The severity of this judgment indicates that God considered it a matter of the utmost priority. In Proverbs the destructive consequences of adultery are clearly described.

> Can one go upon hot coals, and his feet not be burned?
>
> So he that goeth in to his neighbor's wife; whosoever toucheth her shall not be innocent.
>
> Proverbs 6:28, 29

> But whoso committeth adultery with a woman lacketh understanding: he that doeth it destroyeth his own soul.
>
> A wound and dishonour shall he get; and his reproach shall not be wiped away.
>
> vv. 32, 33

In the New Testament the church was to discipline adulterous members by excommunicating them from the assembly.

> It is reported commonly that there is fornication among you, and such fornication as is not so much as named among the Gentiles, that one should have his father's wife.
>
> And ye are puffed up, and have not rather mourned, that he that hath done this deed might be taken away from among you.
>
> For I verily, as absent in body, but present in spirit, have judged already, as though I were present, concerning him that hath so done this deed,
>
> In the name of our Lord Jesus Christ, when ye are gathered together, and my spirit, with the power of our Lord Jesus Christ,
>
> To deliver such an one unto Satan for the destruction of the flesh, that the spirit may be saved in the day of the Lord Jesus.
>
> 1 Corinthians 5:1–5

Christians were not even to fellowship with those living in adultery.

> But fornication, and all uncleanness, or covetousness, let it not be once named among you, as becometh saints;
>
> Neither filthiness, nor foolish talking, nor jesting, which are not convenient: but rather giving of thanks.
>
> For this ye know, that no whoremonger, nor unclean person, nor covetous man, who is an idolator, hath any inheritance in the kingdom of Christ and of God.
>
> Let no man deceive you with vain words; for because of these things cometh the wrath of God upon the children of disobedience.
>
> Be not ye therefore partakers with them.
>
> Ephesians 5:3–7

Paul repeatedly warns Christians to avoid this sin because of its terrible consequences.

Can Adultery Be Forgiven?

Of course, adultery is not the unpardonable sin. God promises to cleanse us from "all unrighteousness."

> If we confess our sins, he is faithful and just to forgive us our sins, and to cleanse us from all unrighteousness.
>
> 1 John 1:9

The church has a sacred obligation toward those who have fallen into this sin. It has the obligation to bring them to spiritual repentence and help them rebuild their lives.

> Brethren, if a man be overtaken in a fault, ye which are spiritual, restore such an one in the spirit of meekness; considering thyself, lest thou also be tempted.
>
> Galatians 6:1

> Bear ye one another's burdens, and so fulfil the law of Christ.
>
> v. 2

We have an obligation to restore them into the fellowship of the church. After the church at Corinth disciplined the immoral brother, he repented. However, the church refused to accept him back. Consequently, Paul wrote further instructions.

> Sufficient to such a man is this punishment, which was inflicted of many.
>
> So that contrariwise ye ought rather to forgive him, and comfort him, lest perhaps such a one should be swallowed up with overmuch sorrow.
>
> Wherefore I beseech you that ye would confirm your love toward him.
>
> 2 Corinthians 2:6–8

The church must preach God's righteous standard of marital fidelity and at the same time, help, counsel, and restore those who have violated that standard. We must never minimize sin or neglect the process of restoring the sinner.

How Can I Maintain Purity in an Age of Moral Impurity?

1. Commit your body and your sexual desires to the Lord.

> I beseech you therefore, brethren, by the mercies of God, that ye present your bodies a living sacrifice, holy, acceptable unto God, which is your reasonable service.
>
> And be not conformed to this world: but be ye transformed by the renewing of your mind, that ye may prove what is that good, and acceptable, and perfect will of God.
>
> Romans 12:1, 2

Perhaps you have been recently separated or divorced. You now are living without the gratification of your sexual desires and at times it is very frustrating. In dealing with people, I know those recently separated or divorced are very vulnerable and oftentimes (in their own mind) excuse sexual immorality on the basis of the fact that they really need it. Seek God's forgiveness and then commit your body and your sexual desires to the Lord.

2. Don't constantly think about sexual immorality, read about it, or watch programs that promote it.

> But I say unto you, That whosoever looketh on a woman to lust after her hath committed adultery with her already in his heart.
>
> Matthew 5:28

In dealing with couples whose marriages have fallen apart, they will often express to me that they began watching an excessive amount of television which promoted the idea of sexual license. They developed an attitude that "everybody else is doing it so why not me?" They also began thinking that they were missing out on life. At a very vulnerable time in their lives they fell into that temptation and sin, and as a result were living with the terrible consequences of it. The Bible speaks of those who have "eyes full of adultery" (2 Peter 2:14).

3. ***Don't constantly talk about immorality and don't joke about it.***

> But fornication, and all uncleanness, or covetousness, let it not be once named among you, as becometh saints;
>
> Neither filthiness, nor foolish talking, nor jesting, which are not convenient: but rather giving of thanks.
>
> Ephesians 5:3, 4

It is so important where we work and in our interpersonal relationships with others that we do not constantly talk about the subject of human sexuality. Whenever that becomes the center of our conversation or we are always telling dirty jokes, the chances are that we are setting ourselves up for a great fall.

4. ***Establish clear boundaries in your physical relationships with others and don't violate them.***

> For this is the will of God, even your sanctification, that ye should abstain from fornication:
>
> That every one of you should know how to possess his vessel in sanctification and honour;
>
> Not in the lust of concupiscence, even as the Gentiles which know not God:

> That no man go beyond and defraud his brother in any matter: because that the Lord is the avenger of all such, as we also have forewarned you and testified.
>
> For God hath not called us to uncleanness, but unto holiness.
>
> 1 Thessalonians 4:3–7

The idea of "defrauding" is the concept of withholding sexual satisfaction. It means to arouse desires in yourself or others which cannot be fully justified outside of the marital relationship. If you are single or divorced and you are establishing a dating relationship, make sure that you commit yourself to clear boundaries in that dating relationship and then don't violate them.

5. *Avoid circumstances where you could be overcome with temptation.*

The Bible tells us to "flee youthful lusts" (2 Timothy 2:22). The story of Joseph has great merit in that after Potiphar's wife tried to seduce him, he fled. Oftentimes, we need to avoid the circumstances and situations in which we can bend to the pressure around us.

Chapter Eight

Children, Single Parents, and Divorce

The rising divorce rate within the church not only raises the issue of our relationship to divorced parents but also raises the issue of our relationships to the children of divorce. The face of the family within the church is undergoing dramatic change. With a divorce rate of around 50 percent in the United States, it is estimated that about 30 percent of all children born in the 1980s will experience a parental divorce before they reach age eighteen.[1] * These statistics are forcing the church to face the reality of ministering to single-parent families and the children of divorce.

How Do Children Respond to a Divorce?

Going through a divorce is a deeply traumatic experience for children. In fact, the effects of divorce upon children are increasingly recognized as a major mental health issue.[2] The initial feelings of rejection, loss, loneliness, helplessness, and

* Source notes are at the end of the chapter.

uncertainty exert a profound emotional toll upon children. Many children have feelings of shame, and some even blame themselves for the divorce. Children attempt to manage these confusing emotions in a number of ways. ". . . by coherence, by denial, by courage, by bravado, by seeking support from others, by keeping in motion, by conscious avoidance."[3] In seeking to counsel and encourage these children, the church must be sensitive to their specific feelings and concerns. The following data was collected from a sample of nine- and ten-year-olds. While these emotions may change according to the age of the child when the divorce occurs, they appear to be representative of most children.

Anger. One of the feelings that seems to dominate children of divorce is an intense anger. In one study of nine- and ten-year-olds, this was observed: "Approximately half of the children in this group were angry at their mothers, the other half at their fathers, and a goodly number were angry at both. Many of the children were angry at the parent whom they thought initiated the divorce, and their perception of this was usually accurate."[4] This anger is often vented in temper tantrums and other aggressive behavior. Often mothers were unprepared for their new role as disciplinarians and were so consumed with their own emotional trials that they felt incapable of helping their children.

Fears and Phobias. While preschool children often worry about hunger and starvation, the children in this sample did not. However, one-fourth of them were worried about "being forgotten or abandoned by both parents."[5] Many were worried that their individual needs were likely to be "overlooked or forgotten"[6] and others "expressed the not wholly unrealistic concern that reliance on one rather than two parents was considerably less secure, and therefore the child's position in the world had become more vulnerable."[7] While some of the fears were real and some imagined, they were nevertheless real in the mind of the child.

Shaken Sense of Identity. Since the self-image of children and the sense of who they are is "closely tied to the external family structure and developmentally dependent on the physical presence of parental figures," they were deeply shaken by the parental breakup.[8] Sometimes this behavior is manifested in acts of stealing and lying.

Loneliness. In divorce children often feel trapped between parents. They feel that the divorce is a battle between the parents and they are forced to take sides. They often feel that to choose one parent is essentially a betrayal of the other parent. Consequently, "paralyzed by their own conflicting loyalties and the severe psychic or real penalties which attach to choice, many children refrained from choice and felt alone and desolate, with no place to turn for comfort or parenting."[9]

School Performance. Half of the children in this study encountered a noticeable decline in school performance after the divorce. The behavior of many children changed when they went to school. Some children who were withdrawn at home became bossy and controlling at school. Others demonstrated a decreased ability to concentrate in class, along with aggressive behavior on the playground.[10] After a year, 75 percent of the children who experienced a decline in school performance had returned to their previous educational and social status.

Parent-Child Relationships. In this study, 26 percent of the children formed a relationship with one parent that essentially excluded the other. "The angers which the parent and the child shared soon became the basis for complexly organized strategies aimed at hurting and harassing the former spouse, sometimes with the intent of shaming him or her into returning to the marriage."[11] Sometimes it was for the purpose of vengeance. Often the child divided his family into the "good" parent and the "bad" parent. On the other hand, many children became more empathetic and understanding of the struggle of their parents, and sometimes took on the responsibility of caring for the younger children in the family.

Do Children Overcome These Emotional Traumas?

The children in this study were analyzed one year after the initial conference to determine how they had responded to the divorce trauma over time. In half of the children, the initial suffering and pain had almost entirely subsided. Although they seemed well adjusted, they still had strong feelings of anger and hostility. The other half gave evidence of troubled and depressive behavior. The initial symptoms persisted and in many cases worsened. "A significant component in this now chronic maladjustment was a continuing depression and low self-esteem, combined with frequent school and peer difficulties."[12]

What Are the Long-Term Effects of Divorce?

The most significant long-term effect of divorce upon children seems to be in the parent-child relationships. One study compared college students from intact families with college students from families who had divorced ten years earlier. The researcher concluded that "the parent-child relationships of these subjects whose families were divorced before they were 11 years old, as contrasted with those in intact families, are characterized as having greater distance, poorer communication, less affection and warmth, and less positive feelings in general."[13] The father-child relationship is crucial to the development of children, yet statistics show that "5 years after the divorce only 30% of the children had an emotionally nurturant relationship with their fathers."[14] Another study of children of divorce noted three separate experiences after several years. About 33 percent of the children survived successfully with positive self-esteem and a good outlook on life. Another third did not recover and continued to suffer from the emotional trauma, hoping that things would eventually return to normal. The other third continued to struggle with some successes and many difficulties.[15]

What is crystal clear from this data is that there are serious short-term and long-term emotional effects of divorce upon children. Nearly all children experience problems when the separation and divorce occurs with nearly two-thirds of them experiencing long-term difficulties. Recently I came across a helpful book on this subject. It is a book written to the parents of divorce in order to help their children. It is written by Judson J. Swihart and Steven L. Brigham and is entitled *Helping Children of Divorce.* In this book they have a very helpful chart that gives some ideas on how to lessen the impact of divorce on children. I've included this chart at the end of the chapter in order to help and assist parents.

What Can Be Done?

In light of the fact that children are the innocent victims of a divorce that they did not want and they often suffer immediate and long-term emotional difficulties, what can be done? Here are a number of suggestions:

1. Parents should consider the impact of separation and divorce upon their children before they act.

I am amazed in dealing with couples who are considering separation and divorce, how little thought and consideration they have given as to how it will affect their children. It is as if they are so consumed with their own problems that they have had little time to deal with their children. Parents should do all that they can to salvage their marriage and keep the relationship together for their own benefit and the emotional and spiritual health of their children.

2. ***The church has a major obligation to single-parent families.***

Those of us who are happily married know little of the frustrations of single-parent families. Often Mom is acting as both mom and dad, as well as the major source of income. Frequently the socioeconomic status of the family goes down after divorce. The overwhelming responsibility of single parenting often limits the time the parent is able to spend with the children and further complicates the difficulties of the children. At this time of frustration and change, the church should provide a sense of stability and security. This can be done in various ways. First, *the local church should be sensitive to the financial needs of the family.* Providing food, presents for special occasions, repair work for the house and car, and financial advice, can meet important physical needs. Second, *the church should help the children.* If they are attending a Christian school, and now (because of the divorce and lack of money) are faced with the prospects of changing schools, the church should provide tuition assistance. The church should assign shepherd families to provide an extended network of friends and role models for the children. Third, and perhaps most important, *the church should accept divorced parents and their children as first-class citizens of the church.* Often the church adds to the shame and embarrassment of these families rather than helping them.

What Are the Problems of Divorcees and Single Parents?

According to *Newsweek,* July 15, 1985, "One out of four households with children is headed by a single parent—and by 1990 the figure could double. The impact on society is only now being measured, but the trend is already redefining our concept of the American family." It is estimated that approximately half of the children born in the 1980s will spend part of their childhood living with one parent. In counseling with parents who have been divorced, I have been deeply touched by the frustrations they encounter, and the fact that the church has for the most part ignored them.

Much of the research on single parents deals with the problems and role adjustments of the mother. This is logical since 87 percent of single families are headed by a woman. However, single families headed by fathers have increased 127 percent since 1970, and the trend should continue (*Psychology Today,* June 1985). New research indicates that although men tend to adjust sooner to the problems of divorce, both men and women encounter some of the same frustrations.[16]

Effect on Women. Divorce dramatically alters the direction of a spouse and a family. Things will never be the same. Divorce sets in motion a series of events that have not been faced by either the parents or children. For women, these events include:

1. Seeking employment if the wife had not been employed.
2. Seeking child-care if she did not already have it.
3. Trying to live on less income, usually, than she had while married.
4. Seeking a relationship with another man.
5. Developing new friendships as her former married friends "drop" her.
6. Assuming responsibility for all aspects of family living.[17]

These events precipitate major emotional, spiritual, financial, and legal problems.

A Deep Sense of Guilt. I believe that Christians who go through divorce carry a great burden of guilt. This guilt initially grows out of a feeling that they have failed. The guilt is compounded by the judgmental attitudes of many Christians. When divorcees go to church, they often feel alienated from the mainstream of the congregation and treated like they have leprosy. Rather than being welcomed with loving and forgiving arms, they are often held at arm's length from the understanding and security they need. I am convinced that a "No Divorce—No Remarriage" position contributes to this legalistic Phariseeism that excludes hurting and suffering people from the healing process that the church is called upon to provide.

A Profound Sense of Failure. In dealing with divorcees I often hear statements like these: "If I had been more considerate, loving, and forgiving, maybe we would not have divorced." In the aftermath of a divorce, people spend considerable time in reflecting on what they should have done in order to prevent the divorce. This adds up to a sense of failure. It also raises the question as to whether the person can ever develop another intimate relationship without failure and the subsequent hurt and bitterness.

Depression and Alienation. Divorced men and women commit suicide at a rate three to four times more often than married men and women. Many divorced people feel that their way of life has ended, and they go through emotional depression accompanied by extreme loneliness. William Good's research identified various factors that contribute to depression in women.

1. *Length of Marriage.* Long-term marriages were associated with more difficulty in adjusting to divorce because of the greater commitment to, and involvement in, the marriage relationship.
2. *Age.* Age was related to greater difficulty in adjusting to divorce, with older women experiencing more ad-

justment problems. The possibilities for establishing a satisfying new life may be more limited for the older woman. She may have greater difficulty reentering the job market, for example.

3. *Number of Children.* The presence of two or more children was associated with more difficulty in adjusting to divorce. The responsibility and concerns of rearing a number of children, especially small children, is often perceived as an awesome burden and can be frightening. There is also a tendency to worry about the effects of divorce upon the children.

4. *Who Suggested the Divorce.* The greatest amount of trauma was suffered by the woman if her husband suggested the divorce. Very likely men would also tend to experience considerable trauma if their wives suggested a divorce. Many persons are disturbed by being the rejected partner.

5. *Decisiveness About the Divorce.* Unsteadiness in the decision was associated with greater difficulty in adjusting to divorce. Indecision about the divorce, or the "on again, off again" approach, creates a strain upon the psychological equilibrium of many individuals and promotes anxiety and insecurity.[18]

Financial Limitations. In general, women tend to suffer greater financial loss after divorce than men. Since most of the single-parent families are headed by women, the children inevitably suffer. One study indicated that five years after the breakup, one-third of the women were struggling daily for economic survival. One-half were maintaining a modest standard of living, and one-fifth were financially secure. After divorce, women are often compelled to work and soon discover the inequities of the job market and their lack of marketable skills.

Some families endure delinquent payments of child support and alimony. All of these factors put strong pressure on the single-parent family.

The Legal Hassles. During the divorce, the couple must face a number of legal issues that often become court battles. Ownership of property, joint checking accounts, child custody, alimony, and visitation rights are some of the major problems that are frequently resolved through lawyers. These conflicts often bring couples into emotional and verbal wars. The legal procedures exact a toll on each person's physical, spiritual, and emotional health.

The Challenge of Being Mom and Dad. Perhaps the greatest frustration of single parenting is the feeling that one has to be both Mom and Dad. This additional responsibility is further complicated by the fact that single parents usually have less time to spend with their children than married parents. By the time they work all day, collect the children from day-care, cook supper, help with homework, and clean the house, it is time for bed and Mom is exhausted. She collapses into bed awaiting the sound of the alarm, which signals the start of the furious routine for another day.

How Should a Christian Respond to the Personal Trauma of Divorce?

The feelings of guilt, failure, depression, and alienation, along with the financial and legal hassles and the challenge of single parenting combine to present an overwhelming challenge and burden for the divorced parents. Christians are not immune from any of these problems. Dr. Edward Hindson, in his book *The Total Family* (Tyndale House, 1980), offers a series of *Don'ts* for divorced and single parents.

1. *Don't blame God for your circumstances (divorced or widowed).*

2. *Don't criticize your divorced partner in front of your children (remember, he or she is still their parent also).*

3. *Don't condemn yourself for circumstances beyond your control.* "I wish I had done better"; "If I had said this, maybe he would not have left"; "If I had only been there, maybe he would not have died."

4. *Don't wish you were someone else (that is irresponsibly avoiding reality).* Such day-dreaming will ruin your kids.

5. *Don't speculate endlessly about what might have been if. . . .* The time has come to fully accept things as they are now. If your partner left and remarried, the Scripture advises not to take him back (*see* Deuteronomy 24:1-4).

6. *Don't overly "spiritualize" your problems.* Your kids will see right through all that drippy talk about how you are really satisfied things worked out the way they did. Don't misquote Romans 8:28.

7. *Don't excuse yourself either.* It takes two to tangle. Don't put all the blame on your partner.

8. *Don't become overly dependent on the wrong people.* Stay away from married men/women. Don't constantly run to your friends with your problems. It will confuse you. Learn to place your greatest dependence on the Lord Himself.

9. *Don't dominate your kids (so they won't turn out like you).* You may drive them off by being too much of a martyr.

10. *Don't worry about the future; trust God.*[19]

That's good advice. Now let me give a series of positive principles that will help people to face the trauma and aftermath of divorce.

Be Honest With Your Feelings. When Christians are angry, hurt, depressed, and so forth, they often try to hide their feelings. "How are you?" someone asks. "Just fine," we respond when in reality our inner world is falling apart. Sometimes people going through a divorce put on a strong front and try to hide their emotions. But you do not bury your emotions dead—you bury them alive, where they continue to destroy your emotional and spiritual health. On the other hand, some Christians are constantly expressing their innermost angers and hurts. They yell at the kids, and those around them. They lash out at everyone. We should neither suppress or express our feelings. Rather we should confess them. The Hebrew word for *confess* means "to agree with." Confessing sin to God is agreeing with God that we have sinned. Confessing our emotions is agreeing with the fact that we are hurting. Be honest with God. Tell Him you are angry—He knows it already. Tell Him you are hurt. Tell Him you are bitter. Tell Him you are depressed. Be honest with God and then ask Him for grace to go on.

After confessing your feelings to God and seeking His help, then you need to find a mature Christian with whom you can discuss your frustrations. Paul reminds us, "Bear ye one another's burdens, and so fulfil the law of Christ" (Galatians 6:2). When two bear the burden, it seems lighter. When two bear the burden, it is not as lonely. However, no one can help you bear your burden unless you are willing to share your burden. Be honest with God and others.

Accept the Forgiveness of God. The only cure for guilt is the forgiveness of God. Since divorce is nearly always the result of failure on the part of both partners, the burden of guilt is at times rather heavy for a divorced Christian. The Christian must then accept the forgiveness of God, and must learn to forgive himself as part of the process of spiritual healing.

> If we confess our sins, he is faithful and just to forgive us our sins, and to cleanse us from all unrighteousness.
>
> 1 John 1:9

God's forgiveness is greater than our sin. Even if you are divorced and remarried on grounds other than those permitted in the Bible, God forgives and forgets. Study, memorize, and meditate on the following verses.

> He hath not dealt with us after our sins; nor rewarded us according to our iniquities.
>
> For as the heaven is high above the earth, so great is his mercy toward them that fear him.
>
> As far as the east is from the west, so far hath he removed our transgressions from us.
>
> Psalms 103:10-12

> In whom we have redemption through his blood, the forgiveness of sins, according to the riches of his grace;
>
> Ephesians 1:7

> I, even I, am he that blotteth out thy transgressions for mine own sake, and will not remember thy sins.
>
> Isaiah 43:25

Learn to Forgive Yourself. Although reconciliation of divorced people is desirable, it is often impossible. You cannot go back and change the past. In your mind you may have identified the things you could have changed that would have prevented the divorce. If you spend all your time pondering the mistakes of the past, you will fail to meet the challenges of the present and the opportunities of the future. Paul gives important advice in Philippians.

> Brethren, I count not myself to have apprehended: but this one thing I do, forgetting those things which are behind, and reaching forth unto those things which are before,
>
> I press toward the mark for the prize of the high calling of God in Christ Jesus.
>
> Let us therefore, as many as be perfect, be thus minded: and if in any thing ye be otherwise minded, God shall reveal even this unto you.
>
> Philippians 3:13–15

God has forgiven you—you must forgive yourself. God has forgotten your past, and so must you.

Develop a Close Personal Relationship With God. Loneliness is a major problem for divorcees. Vernon Brewer is the Dean of Students at Liberty University. Recently he completed a successful battle with cancer. I remember one day, in the midst of his chemotherapy treatments, we were eating lunch together and discussing the loneliness that he frequently faced. He shared with me an important truth that God had taught him. "Ed," he said, "loneliness is our friend if it causes us to enjoy the presence of God more than the fellowship of other human beings." God can use this time of loneliness in your life to draw you closer to Him. Embrace this opportunity to enjoy God's presence. How can you do that?

1. *Read the Bible and pray every day.*
2. *Learn to confess your doubts and fears during the day.*

3. *Learn to pray wherever you are.*

4. *Develop a continual awareness of God's presence.*

Learn to Trust God One Day at a Time. One person wrote and shared with me what God was doing in his life:

> My divorce, along with other things, has caused me to reevaluate my goals and my relationship with God. My desire is to serve God, and I want to dedicate my life fully to that end regardless of any personal sacrifice involved. I am sick of the world's system and seek relief from its demands. I long for the inner peace that comes only from serving God. Obviously, the world system has no lasting value to offer.

The mountain of problems faced by divorced Christians seems insurmountable, but God wants us to live one day at a time. Begin each day by asking for God's wisdom, courage, faith, grace, and strength. Don't be overly concerned with tomorrow or next week. Believe God for today. Robert Schuller, in his book *Tough Times Never Last, But Tough People Do,* states "There will never be another now—I'll make the most of today. There will never be another me—I'll make the most of myself." God has promised to sustain us in every difficulty. At the end of the day, thank God for giving you the grace to survive and then face tomorrow with the promise of more grace for a new day. Paul talks about trusting God in Philippians.

> Be careful for nothing; but in every thing by prayer and supplication with thanksgiving let your requests be made known unto God.
>
> And the peace of God, which passeth all understanding, shall keep your hearts and minds through Christ Jesus.
>
> Philippians 4:6,7

Reach Out and Touch Someone. Don't sit home alone week after week. Develop new friendships. You must take the initiative. The writer of Proverbs states "A man that hath friends must shew himself friendly: and there is a friend that sticketh closer than a brother" (18:24). In counseling with divorced men and women and single parents, many of them have told me that they joined a community self-help group for single parents. They have told me that this was one of the best decisions they made, and it helped them immensely in working through their problems. At Thomas Road Baptist Church, we have similar groups for single parents where they can communicate and encourage each other.

I also encourage people to get involved in helping others. Teach a Sunday-school class. Visit the hospital or nursing home. Attend a Bible study. Take food to a poor family. Christ promised "Blessed are the merciful: for they shall obtain mercy" (Matthew 5:7). Christ promised His blessing for those who were compassionate and caring for the poor and needy. He promised that if we cared and met the needs of others, God would then meet our needs. Reach out and touch someone!

> Wherefore comfort yourselves together, and edify one another, even as also ye do.
>
> Now we exhort you, brethren, warn them that are unruly, comfort the feebleminded, support the weak, be patient toward all men.
>
> See that none render evil for evil unto any man; but ever follow that which is good, both among yourselves, and to all men.
>
> 1 Thessalonians 5:11,14,15

When Should a Christian Remarry?

The issue of remarriage is an important issue for Christians. The Bible permits remarriage on the basis of sexual sin or desertion by the unbeliever. Research indicates that the remarriages of divorced persons are more likely to result in divorce than first marriages. As mentioned earlier, problems that precipitated the first divorce are perpetuated in the remarriage and can contribute to the second divorce. Consequently, it is important to make the right decisions concerning remarriage. If you are considering remarriage or you know a friend who is considering it, then you must address and answer these questions:

Is there a biblical basis for divorce?

Recently someone came to see me to discuss the issue of remarriage. He had listened to the lessons I had taught at Thomas Road Baptist Church and wanted some advice and direction. This person had been divorced several years earlier and had been dating someone for about six months, and they were talking about marriage. I began by asking him to relate to me the grounds for his divorce. He told me that the divorce was on the grounds of incompatibility. His wife was a Christian, and there was no adultery involved, and she had not remarried. After listening carefully to his situation, I shared with him that he did not have a biblical basis for his divorce and, that while he was legally divorced, he was not biblically divorced. Therefore he was not free to date or remarry someone else. He should begin seeking reconciliation with his wife. Needless to say, my advice was not well accepted. He was hoping that I could give him scriptural justification for what he wanted to do.

Reread the chapters on the teaching of Moses, Jesus, and Paul on the subject of divorce. Go back and do it now. Before you begin thinking of dating or remarriage, you must be sure that you have a biblical basis for your divorce.

Is there hope for reconciliation?

Even after separation and divorce, God desires reconciliation.

> And unto the married I command, yet not I, but the Lord,
> Let not the wife depart from her husband:

> But and if she depart, let her remain unmarried, or be reconciled to her husband: and let not the husband put away his wife.
>
> 1 Corinthians 7:10,11

It is not always possible to reconcile. However, each person must do all that he or she can to seek reconciliation. Even if the divorce is on biblical grounds, God can work miracles and restore broken and fragmented families. I remember a number of years ago an unusual thing happened at our commencement at Liberty Baptist College (now Liberty University). The parents of one of our graduates had divorced and they both attended the commencement. They sat in different parts of the auditorium. Both were unsaved. After the commencement address, Dr. Falwell gave a public invitation for people who would like to be saved. This graduate's mom and dad came down separate aisles and met at the altar. They were led to Christ by their son and several months later remarried.

Before a person considers remarriage, he must answer the question, "Have I done what I could to seek reconciliation?" Each person must be assured in his own mind that he has sought reconciliation before considering remarriage. One person wrote me and expressed her ongoing hope for reconciliation.

> Being divorced myself, of course, triggers questions of more than just a casual interest; however, you answered most of my questions. I did not initiate my divorce. I sought reconciliation and resisted the divorce as much as possible. I also learned that there is no power on earth that can stop one person from divorcing another when that person pursues divorce. I still pray for reconciliation and believe that God one day will answer my prayers.

Someone else wrote:

> I have listened to your tapes on "Marriage, Divorce and Remarriage." They have been very meaningful to me and my wife. We were headed for divorce court and now a healing miracle is taking place.

Another person wrote:

> I am a divorced Christian. I was contemplating remarrying when a friend had me listen to your "Marriage, Divorce and Remarriage" tapes.
>
> I found them hard to swallow at first. Admitting what I had done wrong and realizing the cure is even harder did not sit well *at all.*
>
> After six years of separation and divorce I have made a commitment to try and reconcile again with my ex-husband.
>
> My boyfriend and I have broken off our relationship, and for the time being I have moved away to help some feelings heal.
>
> As I try to explain this, many of my non-Christian friends as well as some Christians cannot understand this. Because of your messages and my followup study this has become easier.
>
> Thank you for your dedicated study of God's Word. For bringing out the Truth of God's love for us no matter how difficult it may seem at first.
>
> Each day has taught me to be more dependent on God, to rely on His promises of love and support to give me no more than I can handle.

I received a very moving poem written by a lady whose husband left her. For nine years she prayed for reconciliation, and he came back. I hope and pray that this poem will be an encouragement to those who are seeking reconciliation.

LOVE

Love is a precious thing.
It comes from God above.
If God is not in your love
It's not worth thinking of.

I love the man I married,
But he went away.
That did not kill my love,
It just grew from day to day.

Through those long and lonely years
I prayed this prayer each day.
"God, if he loves me,
Please bring him home today."

It seemed today would never come,
But I never forgot to pray.
Thank God, He answered
In a sweet and humble way.

The man I love returned one day.
I'm so thankful that he did.
He asked me to forgive him,
And this is what I said:
"There is nothing to forgive,
I forgave you day by day,
For every heartbreak you caused me,
While you were away."

I know that I'm not perfect
So this I want to say,
"If I had not forgiven you,
God would not have forgiven me."

The man I love is here today
So this I still can say,
Love is a precious thing,
God brought him home to stay.

God can do things for others
Just like He does for me,
If they will only trust in Him,
For God is love, you see.

Has there been time for spiritual and emotional healing?

We have already discussed the deep emotional and spiritual wounds that result from divorce. These wounds do not heal overnight. When a person brings those hurts to a second relationship, it is often difficult to establish a healthy second marriage. In discussing these emotional bonds, the authors of a book on marriage remind us of the challenges. "Emotional remarriage is the slow, sometimes painful, process by which the divorced person re-establishes the bond of attraction, commitment, and trust with someone. Divorced persons may find the establishment of a new marital-type relationship difficult because they fear failing again and because they have been hurt and disappointed."[20]

Don't date or remarry on the rebound. Because of the loneliness and hurt of divorce, some people date just to fill that void. Their premise for a new relationship with another person is what that person can do for them. This is a poor foundation for a relationship—especially marriage. Marriage is predicated upon a "giving" relationship and not a "taking" one. Divorced persons should allow adequate time for emotional and spiritual healing before developing another intimate friendship that could lead to remarriage.

Is the prospective spouse/date a committed Christian?

There are really two fundamental issues at stake. Is the person you are dating a Christian? Is the person you are dating a committed Christian? I am amazed at how many Christians who are divorced will justify dating an unsaved person by claiming that he/she understands them and is meeting their needs. My advice is always, "Don't date or marry an unsaved person!" The Bible is clear on this issue.

> Be ye not unequally yoked together with unbelievers: for what fellowship hath righteousness with unrighteousness? and what communion hath light with darkness?

> And what concord hath Christ with Belial? or what part hath he that believeth with an infidel?
>
> And what agreement hath the temple of God with idols? for ye are the temple of the living God; as God hath said, I will dwell in them, and walk in them; and I will be their God, and they shall be my people.
>
> Wherefore come out from among them, and be ye separate, saith the Lord, and touch not the unclean thing; and I will receive you.
>
> And will be a Father unto you, and ye shall be my sons and daughters, saith the Lord Almighty.
>
> 2 Corinthians 6:14–18

In addition to being a Christian, I always advise people to date committed Christians—ones who are reading the Bible daily, praying, witnessing, attending church, and so forth. Since you will face major problems in a remarriage, you had better begin by marrying someone who is totally committed to God and His Word. To do less than that is to invite trouble and frustration in the future.

Does the new relationship emphasize mental, emotional, and spiritual intimacy and minimize physical intimacy?

Too often dating relationships are built upon the mutual gratification of sexual needs. I have heard many Christians who are divorced justify sexual intimacy prior to remarriage. Some divorced women have told me that they feel their dates expect such intimacy on their first date! While the abrupt end of sexual intercourse after divorce is a major pressure point, it does not justify sexual gratification outside of the marriage covenant. Couples should discuss setting guidelines for physical intimacy in their dating relationship. I would suggest that you go back and read the chapter on "The Bible, Human Sexuality, and Adultery," chapter 7.

Intimacy can be developed without being controlled primarily by sexual gratification. Develop intellectual, emotional, and spiritual intimacy. Get to know the person—their likes and dislikes, their family, their background, their dreams, their fears, and so forth. Grow together spiritually. Read the Bible and pray together. Share what God is teaching as an individual. Dick Purnell, in his book, *Becoming A Friend and Lover,* gives an excellent definition of intimacy:

> I define true intimacy as total life sharing—sharing your life completely with someone else. It includes being open to and deeply involved in the inner and outer life of another person by seeking to understand all of the aspects that make up that person. Intimacy is a process, not a once-for-all accomplishment. Each of us is developing, growing, learning and aging in all aspects of our lives. Life is in constant flux, so intimacy, if it is in a healthy state, is not static but constantly developing and growing, too.[21]

He goes on to state:

> The five major areas of life can be defined as the social, emotional, mental, physical, and spiritual. These can be represented by a five-pointed star. Knowing only one or two of these areas of another person's makeup leaves a very lopsided impression of who that person is. To be intimate with someone, we must share joys and sorrows, ups and downs, likes and dislikes and the strengths and weaknesses in each of these areas. In this way we can know them and be known by them as true people, not as facades or fakes. Through mutual caring, giving and accepting of the person as he or she truly is, we both grow.[22]

I would challenge those who are dating and considering remarriage to develop their intimacies without the domination of sexual indulgence.

What About Children and Stepparents?

According to many of the couples I have talked with, the major problem in remarriage is the rearing of children who are not their own. Being stepparents and relating to stepchildren is a unique challenge that often frustrates both the parents and the children. There are a number of interesting findings in regard to children and stepparents.

1. Stepchildren more often express a preference for one parent or the other (either the stepparent or their biological parent) than do children who live with both biological parents.

2. Children perceive that their stepparents discriminate against them more often than their biological parents and that stepparents of the opposite sex discriminate against them the most. Children feel that the stepmother discriminates against them more often than the stepfather.

3. Female children involved in remarriages express feelings of being rejected by parents more often than do male children.

4. Both male and female children involved in remarriages more often desire to emulate their biological parent rather than a stepparent.[23].

The following advice should be heeded.

1. Encourage children to form new relationships with their stepfamily. Special activities that bring stepchildren together with the stepparent are important in developing communication and building a caring environment.

2. Don't criticize either natural parent or anyone else in the family in the presence of the child. This only intensifies a sense of insecurity and instability.

3. Be courteous and kind in your relationship with your ex-spouse. Don't put the child in the crossfire of an angry and hostile relationship.

4. It is important for children to maintain a relationship with their natural parent. Don't force this relationship but encourage its development.

5. Don't require major changes in the child's routine or behavior.

6. The natural parent should give special attention to the child. It is important that the natural parent and child spend quality time alone.

7. Don't compare child and stepchildren. Treat them with equal dignity and understanding.

8. Promote a family environment that will minimize sexuality. Assist the children in controlling their sexual attractions to each other.

9. Communicate with your spouse in regard to family discipline.

10. Allow the child to decide what he wants to call the stepparent. To force him to use "dad" or "mom" against his will may be perceived as a betrayal of his natural parents.

11. Read carefully the advice given in the next chapter (chapter 9). This chapter deals with the foundational

principles of building a successful family. They apply to remarriage as well as first time marriage. Discuss the principles with your spouse. Discuss the section dealing with children with your family. Remember, it takes time to develop a loving and caring family.

David Hocking, in his book *Marrying Again,* adds a Christian perspective for stepparents.

> The day the children hear that one of their parents is leaving is devastating to them. If often takes years for them to recover. The hurt is deep and carries over into relationships with stepparents. The real needs of the children must be dealt with on a daily basis. Many remarried couples have testified to the terrible home situations that have been created by rebellious stepchildren. You can't run away from these problems. If the stepchildren are in your home, they need your love and attention. It takes God's grace and strength to deal with children who are not your own but are now living with you in your home.
>
> Parents must learn to seek wisdom from God's Word. We need to spend time in prayer, seeking God's help. It is not easy, but God's power and love can meet every situation we face. There needs to be open communication between stepparents and stepchildren; they need to face their inability to cope with situations and be willing to work for peace and harmony in the home by committing themselves to God and His Word for direction and guidance.[24]

Conclusion

Both divorce and remarriage have a profound impact upon children and parents. These life-changing events and their consequences cannot be ignored by the Christian church. Somehow we must extend a helping hand to these hurting people. We can no longer ignore their profound hurt and at times

Divorce Adjustment Factors

Lessens Impact	Increases Impact of Divorce
1. Parents do not put children in the middle.	1. Children are asked to choose between parents.
2. Children are told about the separation.	2. Children are not told about separation or are given little information.
3. Children are aware of the conflict between parents.	3. Parents hide conflict and angry feelings.
4. Children are not held responsible for the divorce.	4. Children are made to feel that divorce is their fault.
5. Children are not used for parental support.	5. Parent relies on child for personal support.
6. Children receive support from significant people.	6. Children are isolated from family friends.
7. Parents resolve personal anger.	7. Parents are unable to resolve anger.
8. The absent parent stays in contact with the child.	8. The absent parent has little contact with child.
9. Siblings.	9. Only child.
10. Family moves into new schedule fairly quickly.	10. Family remains disorganized long after separation.
11. Other environmental factors remain stable.	11. Life is greatly changed: school, neighborhood, parent's work hours and so on.
12. Each parent frequently spends individual time with each child.	12. Little individual attention is given to children.
13. Parents assist each child with individual adjustment reaction.	13. Parents are not aware of individual adjustment reactions.
14. Children are allowed to grieve.	14. Loss is denied—no grieving is allowed.
15. Family focuses on the positive and the future.	15. Family focuses on present calamity.
16. Parents had previous good relationship with child.	16. Child had not previously felt loved or valued by parents.

Judson J. Swihart and Steven L. Brigham, *Helping Children of Divorce,* InterVarsity Press: Downers Grove, Illinois, 1982, p. 39.

their sense of rejection by the Christian community. At a time when they need our support, we must not hesitate to reach out and love them. May God give us the courage to do it and the wisdom to do it right.

Source Notes for Chapter 8 "Children, Single Parents, and Divorce"

1. M. A. Fine, J. R. Moreland, and A. I. Schwebel, "Long-term Effects of Divorce on Parent-Child Relationships," *Developmental Psychology,* vol. 19 (5), 1983, p. 703.
2. *See* "Mental Health Interventions in Divorce Proceedings," *American Journal of Orthopsychiatry,* 48 (2), April 1978.
3. J. S. Wallerstein and J. B. Kelly, "The Effects of Parental Divorce," *American Journal of Orthopsychiatry,* 46(2), April 1976, p. 258.
4. Ibid., p. 260.
5. Ibid., p. 262.
6. Ibid.
7. Ibid.
8. Ibid., p. 263.
9. Ibid., p. 264.
10. Ibid., p. 265.
11. Ibid., p. 266.
12. Ibid., p. 269.
13. M. A. Fine, J. R. Moreland, and A. I. Schwebel, "Long-Term Effects of Divorce on Parent-Child Relationships," *Developmental Psychology,* vol. 19 (5), 1983, p. 710.
14. Ibid., p. 704.
15. J. Wallerstein and J. Kelly, "Children and Divorce: A Review," *Social Work,* November 1979, pp. 468–75.
16. *See* E. E. LeMasters and John DeFrain, *Parents in Contemporary Society* (Homewood, Illinois: The Dorsey Press, 1983), pp. 179–80.
17. Nick Stinnett, James Walters, and Evelyn Kaye, *Relationships in Marriage and the Family* (New York: Macmillan Publishing Co., 1977), p. 132.

18. Ibid., pp. 435–36.
19. Edward E. Hindson, *The Total Family* (Wheaton, Illinois: Tyndale House, 1980), pp. 114–15.
20. Stinnett, Walters, and Kaye, *Relationships in Marriage,* p. 443.
21. Dick Purnell, *Becoming a Friend and Lover* (San Bernardino, California: Here's Life Publishers, 1986), p. 97.
22. Ibid.
23. Stinnett, Walters, and Kaye, *Relationships in Marriage,* p. 447.
24. David Hocking, *Marrying Again* (Old Tappan, N.J.: Fleming H. Revell Company, 1983), pp. 63, 64.

Chapter Nine

The Family: Building on the Right Foundation

The American family is under pressure. Recent statistics indicate that 40 percent of all new marriages will end in divorce, and over 60 percent of these will involve children. As also mentioned earlier, it is estimated that 30 percent of all children born in the 1980s will experience parental divorce before they reach the age of 18. The Christian family is not immune to this breakdown of the family unit. The tragedy is that the church has tended to ignore Christians who have been divorced and/or remarried. Little attention is given to their needs and at times they are driven from the security of Christian fellowship and forced to walk alone. In this chapter I want to discuss the biblical principles for successful family living. If you have been divorced and remarried, or you are considering remarriage, then it is vital that you build your new relationship on the right foundation. If you are considering separation or divorce, then you and your spouse need to read and discuss this chapter in depth. Begin by reading the following passage of Scripture.

> Submitting yourselves one to another in the fear of God.
>
> Wives, submit yourselves unto your own husbands, as unto the Lord.
>
> For the husband is the head of the wife, even as Christ is the head of the church: and he is the saviour of the body.
>
> Therefore as the church is subject unto Christ, so let the wives be to their own husbands in every thing.
>
> Husbands, love your wives, even as Christ also loved the church, and gave himself for it;
>
> That he might sanctify and cleanse it with the washing of water by the word,
>
> That he might present it to himself a glorious church, not having spot, or wrinkle, or any such thing; but that it should be holy and without blemish.
>
> So ought men to love their wives as their own bodies. He that loveth his wife loveth himself.
>
> For no man ever yet hated his own flesh; but nourisheth and cherisheth it, even as the Lord the church:
>
> For we are members of his body, of his flesh, and of his bones.
>
> For this cause shall a man leave his father and mother, and shall be joined unto his wife, and they two shall be one flesh.
>
> This is a great mystery: but I speak concerning Christ and the church.
>
> Nevertheless let every one of you in particular so love his wife even as himself; and the wife see that she reverence her husband.
>
> Ephesians 5:21–33

Paul begins this chapter with "be ye therefore followers [mimics, or imitators] of God, as dear children." Then he goes on to tell us how we can do this. Verses 1–7, walk in love, not lust. Verses 8–14, walk in light, not darkness. Verses 15–21, walk in wisdom, not foolishness. But from verse 22 and following, while the theme remains the same (follow God), the environment in which I am to demonstrate that theme changes. Paul moves from my relationship to self to my relationship with other people. If I am to be a follower of God, how will it affect my family? How will it affect my job? Paul speaks specifically to wives, to husbands, to children, to parents, to employers, to employees, and he translates the principles of Christian living into the home and the workplace.

Wives and Other Missing Links in the Chain of Command

Paul begins with advice to wives. There are two key thoughts in this passage concerning the wife. First, he says: "Wives, submit" (*see* vv. 22, 24). Then he says, ". . . see that she reverence her husband" (v. 33).

Submission

Much confusion exists today over this idea of submission. It does not mean that the wives (or women generally) are inferior to the man. It does not imply inferiority of the person or of her position. Somehow, the position of the mother does not seem to be as important to many as the position of the father. This false impression, unfortunately, has also very often been reinforced in our pulpits.

The biblical pattern is given in 1 Corinthians 11:3: "But I would have you know, that the head of every man is Christ; and the head of the woman is the man; and the head of Christ is God." The principle is the same as that given in Ephesians 5, but here Paul extends the line to include Christ and God. This is very instructive, for it tells us that the idea of inferiority is entirely absent from his thinking. Is God superior to Christ? Is Christ inferior to God? The answer is no. Such a suggestion is heresy. Jesus Christ is co-equal to the Father. He is God of very

God. What, then is the point? There is a difference of *function.* So it is in the family. There is an equality of the persons, but there is a diversity of function within that marital relationship. Just as Christ is subordinate to the Father without being inferior, the woman is subordinate to her husband without that denoting inferiority.

Then, too, submission does not imply an absolute unconditional submission to the husband. There are those who teach the "chain-of-command." God, the husband, the wife, fifteen children, then the dog, the cat, and so forth. The teaching goes something like this: Whatever your husband tells you to do, you are obliged to do it unconditionally. Some even imply that if your husband asks you to commit adultery with somebody in his company, you ought to do it. You are not responsible. If your husband wants you to lie on the telephone, then you must lie. Your husband is accountable for the decisions he makes. You are responsible to obey him. This may sound absurd, but we have actually had instances of this extreme come through our counseling center. Such a teaching is a serious perversion of the biblical principle of submission.

The apostle Peter realized that even in relation to civil authority there comes a time when we must "obey God, rather than men" (Acts 5:29). All of us must give an account of ourselves to God. So when we talk of submission, we are not talking about a blind subservience that violates the principles of Scripture and excuses itself on the basis that somehow the man or the husband will answer to God.

Finally, biblical submission is not to be exercised through intimidation. The problem of battered wives has received a great deal of attention recently. This is a problem, unfortunately, in Christian homes as well. Men assert their authority through verbal or physical abuse. If the wife refuses to obey every demand there is physical violence or mental and emotional abuse. Submission is secured through intimidation. I advise women in such situations to leave immediately and seek sanctuary from the nearest Christian friend until the husband has sought counseling, and the problem is resolved. This seems to be precisely what Peter is referring to in 1 Peter 3:6, "Even as Sarah obeyed Abraham, calling him lord: whose daughters ye are, as long as ye do well, and are not afraid with any amazement" [literally, "terror"]. The wife is to submit to her husband, as Sarah submitted to Abraham, because she respects him, not because she is terrified of him. Scripture never compels the wife to remain in an environment where she or the children are in danger.

The Principle of Mutual Submission. What then is involved in Paul's teaching on submission? There are two predominent emphases. The first is the principle of mutual submission (Ephesians 5:21). I do not believe that the wife has any more obligation to submit to the husband than the husband does to the wife. Within the marital relationship, the wife submits to the husband and the husband to the wife. There is a coming together that builds the right environment and the right relationship for a successful family.

This principle is also taught in 1 Corinthians 7:1–5. There Paul says first: ". . . It is good for a man not to touch a woman. Nevertheless, to avoid fornication, let every man have his own wife, and let every woman have her own husband." That statement alone contradicts the *Playboy, Penthouse* philosophy that women are nothing more than sex symbols for the gratification of the male. Every man has his own wife, and every woman has her own husband. He recognizes the mutual needs of the man and the woman. While Paul is writing at a time when women were not first-class citizens, he puts both in a relationship of equality. He goes on: "Let the husband render unto the wife due benevolence: and likewise also the wife unto the husband." Do you see the mutual obligations one to the other? The wife's body belongs to the husband. Likewise, the husband's body belongs to the wife. In other words, in the marriage vow, there is a mutual giving of two equal persons to one another. Then he says, "Defraud ye not one the other, except it be with consent for a time . . . ." The idea is, do not hold back in sexual relationships that which the partner desires.

The Principle of Voluntary Submission. The second predominant thrust of Paul's teaching on submission is that it is to be voluntary. There must be a willingness on the part of both to submit one to the other and then ultimately to the leadership of God in their lives. But this principle cuts even deeper than this. "For this cause shall a man leave his father and mother, and shall be joined unto his wife, and they two shall be one flesh." (Ephesians 5:31). Have you ever wondered why the Scriptures emphasize, in regard to the first family, ". . . they were both naked, the man and his wife . . ." (Genesis 2:25)? It not only implies the innocence of the environment without sin, it speaks of a vulnerability to one another in the marital relationship. There is a complete openness. For the marriage to work there must be a stripping away of all the facades. Two people see each other as God does, as they really are. This can only come about through a mutual and voluntary submission to one another.

Reverence

The second principle governing Paul's teaching to wives is *reverence.* "Nevertheless, let every one of you in particular so love his wife even as himself; and the wife see that she reverence her husband" (Ephesians 5:33). There are two possible meanings of this word *reverence* (Greek, *phobe* "phobia"). One means to be afraid, or to be frightened. I have been in homes where the wife is petrified to open her mouth. She walks around in fear and trembling; frightened that she might do the wrong thing or say the wrong thing. Nothing is more pitiful than this. A woman, created in the image of God, full of creativity, gifted of God by the Holy Spirit, beaten down by a husband who is too insecure to give her her rightful place in the home, is a travesty.

This word, *reverence,* as used here does not mean "fright." Actually, the term is often used in Scripture, of fearing God (*see* 1 Peter 2:17). We respect God. We reverence Him for who He is; for what He has done in our lives. The wife is to respect her husband. This is not a *forced* respect but an *earned* respect. It comes about as the husband takes the spiritual leadership in the home. He loves his wife as himself and loves as Christ the church. When the husband fulfills his biblical role and is consistent in his life-style, then the logical consequences of that life-style will be a deep respect from his wife.

Nothing is more important in a marriage than respect. Once you lose this, the marriage is headed for a breakdown, if not a breakup. As in athletics, if a team loses respect for the coach, it does not matter how talented they are, the unity, the cohesiveness, and the commitment necessary to win are gone.

Biblical subordination has nothing to do with superiority and domination but has everything to do with respect. Thus Paul's advice is twofold: *submit* and *reverence.* It is a submission that is both mutual and voluntary. It is a reverence that is properly due to the husband who exercises godly leadership in his home, and thus earns respect from his wife, who willingly submits to it. As we will see, for a marriage and family to survive, it is necessary for each member to submit to the leadership of God in his life. It can never depend on one member alone.

Husbands Are for Loving

While the responsibility of the wife is to submit and reverence her husband, the obligation of the husband is leadership and love. "For the husband is the head of the wife" (Ephesians 5:23). We have already noted that this does not mean superiority. Just as there is an equality of persons in the Godhead, with a diversity of function, so it is in the marital relationship. The fact that the husband is the head and the wife needs to submit, does not imply that somehow the wife is inferior. Nor does it imply a dictatorship. But what does it mean? It means first of all, *direction.*

Direction

"For the husband is the head of the wife, even as Christ is the head of the church" (v. 23). Christ directs the church. Leadership means that the husband is going to give direction to the relationship—spiritual leadership, financial leadership, emotional leadership. He is going to take the direction and build the relationship the way it ought to be. Sometimes this leadership will involve applying Scripture directly to family situations. But more often than not it will involve modeling a biblical life-style in the home. A student once told me that her earliest remembrances of her father were of getting up early in the morning and seeing him on his knees in the family room. She remembered him first as a man of God. What a man lives will have far more impression upon his family than what he might say during family devotions.

Direction is the unique responsibility of the man in the marital relationship. This is not to say that the woman has nothing to say about spiritual matters—remember, marriage is a *partnership.* It does mean that she should be able to expect her husband to provide direction, so they can grow together in the Lord.

Leadership also involves *protection.* ". . . and Christ is the saviour [literally, "protector") of the body" (*see* v. 23). Christ is the One who protects us from Satan, from the one who would seek to destroy our relationship with God. So it is in the home. The husband must not only take spiritual direction, but he must also take the role of protecting the relationship. He must not allow anything externally or internally to destroy the health and stability of the marriage.

Leadership issues in a response. "Therefore, as the church is subject to Christ, so let the wives be to their own husbands in every thing" (v. 24). The submission of which Paul is speaking is not a submission based on obligation. It is rather a submission based on love. Why do we obey God? First John 5 tells us we obey Him because we love Him (v. 3). Godly submission to the leadership of the husband is submission that grows out of love and respect for that leadership.

Love

The second key principle is *love.* "Husbands, love your wives, even as Christ also loved the church and gave himself for it; That he might sanctify and cleanse it with the washing of water by the word, That he might present it to himself a glorious church, not having spot, or wrinkle, or any such thing; but that it should be holy and without blemish" (Ephesians 5:25–27). There are two things about the love of Christ evident here. Number One, it was a *costly* love. Even as Christ loved the Church and gave Himself for it. It was a *sacrificial* love. It demanded something of Christ. If you want to really build a relationship on love, it is going to cost something—sacrifice, effort, pain. It may require change. It requires a constant and continual effort in order to maintain the love in that relationship. It costs you something to do it. Marriage is something you have to work at.

Number Two, it is a consistent love. It says that Christ loved us all the way to the point where one day He will present us faultless before Him, holy and without blemish. It was a love that began at Calvary. But He still loves us. And He will love us tomorrow. He will love us until the Day of Christ (Philippians 1:6). This suggests that the marital relationship involves loving—every single day—two people working at loving one another.

If you are going to make marriage work you need a love that will sustain you through the years. It is a love that requires constant effort, constant work. But what does it mean to love? Ephesians 5 gives us six principles.

Love Is Giving. "Husbands, love your wives, even as Christ also loved the church, and gave himself for it" (v. 25). What is love? It is giving. It is giving myself to the person I love. It is really quite simple. Love is giving time. Love is giving an ear. Loving is giving a hand. Love is giving support. It is a smile, a nod, a touch.

When couples are dating, they cannot wait till they see each other to communicate their love. It is wonderful. Somehow, after marriage this often changes. I have talked with husbands who have not told their wives they love them since they were married. He says: "Well, she knows I love her. I go to work. I provide. I pay the bills. I even let her buy a new dress. Of course she knows I love her." Love is a gift. It is a gift that must be given. The husband should tell his wife he loves her every day.

Love Is Caring. "So ought men to love their wives as their own bodies" (v. 28). It is not that I am so in love with my own body but that I am to love my wife "as being" my own body—as being one. Just as a person is interested in taking care of himself, so he ought to be interested in taking care of his wife. You will not know how to care for your wife unless you know her needs. The only way you can know her needs is to listen. I am convinced that what we need to learn more than anything else, as husbands, is the art of listening.

Love Is Growing. "For no man ever yet hated his own flesh; but nourisheth it" (v. 29). The word *nourisheth* means to bring someone to maturity. As the body eats and receives physical nourishment, it is enabled to grow to maturity. I knew that I was in love when Lorna and I married, but I can honestly tell you that I am more in love with her now than ever before. Love grows. As you learn more about your partner, and give, and that person gives to you; as you serve God together and as children come along, love grows.

Love Is Showing. "But nourisheth and cherisheth it" (v. 29). The word *cherish* means to show tender affection and love. Love is showing tender affection. I do not mean a gross kind of public affection. I have discovered through counseling people that oftentimes the married couple who display the most public affection are merely covering up for the fact that deep inside they are far apart. Love is holding her hand, putting your arm around her, hugging her. It is just saying, "I love you." Love is showing tender affection.

Love Is Cleaving. "For this cause shall a man leave his father and mother, and shall be joined unto his wife" (v. 31). As mentioned earlier, the Old Testament Hebrew term for *cleave* means "to be glued together." This is commitment. The reason so many marriages are falling apart is that there is a lack of commitment. When you stood at the marriage altar and said, "I do," you said it *for better or for worse. For richer or poorer. In sickness and in health. Till death do us part.* You made a commitment. Beyond giving, and caring, and growing and sharing, love is a commitment. It is saying that by God's grace and by God's help, no matter how far apart we are, I am committed to making it work.

Love Is Uniting. "For we are members of his body, of his flesh, and of his bones" (v. 30). Paul says, spiritually we have become a part of Christ. We are His Body. So it is in the marital relationship. I leave father and mother and I make a commitment to enter into a one-flesh relationship with another. It is no longer "me." It is "us." It is no longer "you." It is "us." It is no longer "I." It is "we." It is one flesh. Most commentators interpret this to mean physical union. I don't think it should be limited to this. It means that when we mutually submit one to the other; when we make that covenant to live together as husband and wife; and when we are joined, and God seals that union, we become one flesh. Two individuals, yes. But one, in Christ. That means that it is no longer "my house," it is "our house." It is no longer "my ministry," it is "our ministry." It is not "my children," but "our children." It is not "my future," but "our future." It is an equal partnership. It involves praying together over family matters and coming to decisions together. Yes, the husband has the responsibility to give direction, protection, and leadership. Yes, he is to love his wife, and give, and care, and grow, and show, and cleave, and have commitment. But together, he and his wife, serve the Lord.

Parenting

> Children, obey your parents in the Lord: for this is right.
>
> Honour thy father and mother; which is the first commandment with promise.
>
> That it may be well with thee, and thou mayest live long on the earth.
>
> And, ye fathers, provoke not your children to wrath, but bring them up in the nurture and admonition of the Lord.
>
> Ephesians 6:1–4

Children are to obey and honor their parents. But the key to bring this about is what Paul says to the parents. He says: *Do not provoke your children to wrath, but train them in the nurture and admonition of the Lord.*

Do Not Plant Seeds of Bitterness

The first responsibility of parents is given in the form of a negative command: Do not provoke your children to wrath. Put simply, this means we must take great care not to live or speak in such a way before our children that we bring a deep-seeded anger in their life. Do not make them bitter. Parents make mistakes. At the outset, let's realize that no one is perfect, let alone a perfect parent. We are all sinners, some of us saved by grace. We will do and say things that will anger our children. Paul is not asking the impossible. The tense of the verb shows us that what he is saying is, do not be constantly provoking your children to anger. What do parents do to provoke such a response in their children?

First, *by showing favoritism.* If you want to guarantee that your child will live in anger and bitterness and frustration, show favoritism to one child over another. A classic example of favoritism in a family is given in Genesis 25. It is said that Isaac loved Esau, but Rebekah loved Jacob. Such favoritism ultimately led to division in the family. The same thing happened with Joseph. His father loved him above all the other brothers. He was the favorite son. It was given to him a coat of many colors to signify the favor and love of his father. What happened? One day the rest of the brothers, in anger and hatred, sold Joseph into slavery, which would ultimately lead him to Egypt. All of that anger and jealousy was a result of favoritism. Don't provoke your children to wrath.

You can also provoke your children to wrath *by neglecting them.* The story is told in 2 Samuel 14 of David and his son Absalom. Absalom had tried to usurp the throne and was willing even to kill his own father to accomplish it. What caused such hatred and division in David's family? It is reported in verse 28 that Absalom dwelled two full years in Jerusalem without ever laying eyes on the king's face. David did not even take the time to so much as speak with his son. We know later when Absalom was killed, how much David loved him. One of the problems which led Absalom to ultimately usurp the throne was the fact that he perceived that his father had no time for him. I have talked to so many preachers' children and missionaries' children who have told me repeatedly, "My dad had time for the church, for soul winning, for study. He had time for everybody in the church but he had no time for me." They have to work through anger and hurt and bitterness due to years of neglect. This is tragic.

Parents can also provoke their children to wrath by *overprotecting* them. I have seen parents in restaurants, from the time they walk in till the time they walk out, who are constantly reproaching their children for one thing or another. *Don't touch this. Don't touch that. Don't move. Sit up. Sit down.* It is a constant barrage of rebukes. The child gets frustrated. You can overdiscipline your child to the point where the only communication you have with him is negative. This eventually provokes anger and bitterness.

You can provoke your children to wrath by *discouraging* them. A child's self-image is so sensitive. I know in talking to many the struggles they have had to overcome a negative self-image. Many times as a result of what their parents have said to them, they have had to live in loneliness, discouragement, and fear. I shudder when I hear parents tell their children that they are stupid, or clumsy, or dumb, or lazy. They may do a lot of stupid things; they may trip, or do clumsy things, but if the parent keeps telling them that they *are* what they *do,* eventually they become convinced that they have nothing to contribute to life, and commit themselves to failure.

Then there is the opposite extreme. You can provoke your children to wrath by *overinflated ideas* about who they are and what they can do. You build them up to the heights. Many times this is because we get so ego-involved with them. Their successes become our successes. Their failures are ours. Many times we drive them to achieve far beyond their capacities. When the reality of the world confronts them, they become discouraged and shattered. We must be very careful.

You can provoke your children to wrath by *legalism.* You can set so many rules and regulations that ultimately the children are provoked to bitterness. Rules are important to character building. But we need to remind ourselves that they are means to an end—not ends in themselves. Sometimes the rules need to be set aside to give attention to the person. Parents must be extremely careful here to remember that the ultimate goal is to grow children into responsible adults for whom the rules have matured into a value system.

What happens when parents provoke their children to wrath? Colossians 3:21 instructs us that they become discouraged. They lose heart. It is possible to treat children in such a way that their energy, their desire, their feel for living is broken. Although they may outwardly conform to the rules, inside they are listless. They lack the inner drive and dynamics for life. A student once asked Dr. Howard Hendricks, "What do you think about the idea that we should break the will of the child, but not the spirit?" His terse response was, "I don't believe in breaking anything in a child." Do not cultivate a root of bitterness in your children. Nurture them and cultivate in them the Word and the grace of God. This leads us to Paul's second command to parents.

Train and Nurture the Child

The second part of Paul's command is to "bring them up in the nurture and admonition of the Lord" (Ephesians 6:4). Just as we take time and effort to nourish the body, as parents we must take time and energy to nurture our children. The word *nurture* implies "educate." How are we to educate our children?

We train our children *by example.* This first point is the foundation upon which the rest is built. I train my child by my own example. Research now allows us to know that a child's concept of God is identical to his concept of his father. Earthly fathers are linked in the minds of their children to the heavenly Father. When a father lives the wrong example in the home, he perverts the child's concept of God. When he lives a proper and biblical example, he reflects God in the home. This is an awesome responsibility. How much of God is reflected in your life—the life your children see every day in the home?

We train *by instruction.* "Train up a child," the Scripture says, "in the way he should go: and when he is old, he will not depart from it" (Proverbs 22:6). Many interpret this verse to suggest that if you train a child and teach him the Word of God, when he grows up you can be certain he will not depart from the faith. This would be wonderful if it were true. But this is simply not the case. Every generation is responsible before God to accept or reject His Son; to obey or rebel against His Word (Ezekial 18:1–4). There is nothing a parent or anyone else can do to guarantee a positive response to the Word of God from the child. So what is Proverbs 22:6 really teaching? We are to train our children, as in Deuteronomy 6, through prayer, love, and concern. Our responsibility is not to save our children—that's God's work. Rather, we should be nurturing them in the Word of God—cultivating in them those spiritual principles which will, later in life, form the backbone of their value system. We must pray and work and labor and trust God that somehow, in spite of our weaknesses and mistakes, God will honor our commitment. Remember, God had one family, Adam and Eve. He put them in a perfect environment, and they sinned, plunging the human race into sin. I would suggest that if God had a family in a perfect environment, and *they* sinned, how much more likely is it that in an imperfect environment, in spite of our prayers and love, the day may come when the child will decide to go his own way!

I remember a prominent pastor telling about one of his children. When he became a high school senior, despite his parents' instruction, he was going to go his own way. His father simply said to him, "Well, son, you know what I think of that. You know what your mother and I have taught you. I cannot stop you, but I can promise you one thing. Every time you go out, your mom and I are going to sit here in the den and pray for you the whole time you are gone. We will pray that the Holy Spirit will convict you and make you miserable. We will pray that He will, somehow, teach you what you should do." When the boy would go places and do things he knew were wrong, he was so haunted and bothered because he knew his mom and dad were praying for him. Ultimately he repented and committed his life to the Lord.

Then, we train by *correction.* The time will come when you will have to say to a child, "You have crossed a line, and there are certain things we are going to have to do." There are five questions that I have found extremely helpful in a discipline situation. Most children are able to understand these questions when discipline is demanded.

First, *What did you do?* Most of us, when children disobey ask, "Why did you do that?" Of course the child never has an answer. The question is totally irrelevant and entirely unhelpful. Rather you need to ask, "What did you do?" It is important for the child to verbalize out loud what he did.

Second, *Was it right or wrong?* The child must face up to the moral obligation. This is always a very difficult question for the child to answer. This is even worse than admitting what he did. Now he is forced to qualify his behavior. Do not let him off the hook. Do not allow him to try to justify his behavior. Sin always must be faced squarely in order to be dealt with.

Third, *What do you think I ought to do about it?* For the child, this is a terrible question. What should the punishment be? Children are often much more severe on themselves than the parent would be. I hesitate sometimes to ask this because I am thinking of a lesser penalty, and they are automatically thinking of the worst.

Fourth, *What other options did you have?* This is what you did. You have told me that it was wrong. You have told me what we should do about it. Now, looking back on the situation, what could you have done differently? *What were the options?* This question forces him to think through the situation objectively and to verbalize a more constructive approach for the future.

Fifth, *If this happens again, what will you do next time?* This enables the child to link the lesson he has just learned to future circumstances.

By asking these five questions discipline becomes more than just punishment. It becomes a learning experience. It becomes a corrective measure.

Finally, we train *by confirming our love.* It does not matter what the child has done. He is still your child. You must love him regardless of his behavior. It is easiest to love a child when he behaves correctly. It becomes more difficult when he misbehaves. What do you do when you receive a call from the police station and are told that your son is in jail? What do you do when your daughter tells you she is pregnant out of wedlock? Do you look for ways to cover all this up, or do you look for ways to help the child? I have heard some parents say: "Well, don't send them back home to us. He is not my son any longer." I am glad God doesn't treat us that way. God loves with an eternal love—an unconditional love. We are to love our children in spite of what they do and the mistakes and failures and sins of their lives. We wrap our arms around them and say, "You are still my child, and I love you."

To Children:
(How to Raise Happy, Healthy Parents)

Children, obey your parents in the Lord: for this is right.

Honour thy father and mother; which is the first commandment with promise.

Ephesians 6:1,2

Many books on family living deal with husbands, wives, and parents but seldom address the responsibilities of children. I'm convinced that children can have a positive or negative impact on the health and success of a family. David emphasizes the positive influence of children in the family.

> Behold, how good and how pleasant it is for brethren to dwell together in unity!
>
> Psalms 133:1

When brothers and sisters get along with each other ("dwell together in unity"), the home environment is pleasant. On the other hand, God commanded a severe penalty for children who were disruptive and rebellious and had a negative influence on the home.

> If a man have a stubborn and rebellious son, which will not obey the voice of his father, or the voice of his mother, and that, when they have chastened him, will not hearken unto them:
>
> Then shall his father and his mother lay hold on him, and bring him out unto the elders of his city, and unto the gate of his place.
>
> Deuteronomy 21:18,19

Ten Ways Children Can Have a Positive Influence. In talking to teenagers and children, I often remind them that they have a responsibility to rear happy, healthy parents. Let me give you ten ways that children can have a positive influence on the home. (I'm going to discuss these concepts as if I were talking to teenagers and children.) As a parent, you may want to make a list of these ten ideas and put them on the door of your refrigerator.

*1. **Listen to your parents.*** Solomon writes: "My son, hear the instruction of thy father, and forsake not the law of thy mother" (Proverbs 1:8). Listen to your parents. Since parents are older than their children, they have wisdom and insight which children do not have. When I was a teenager, I wasn't all that sure that my parents were all that smart. But after college and now as a parent myself, I am thoroughly convinced that I should have listened more often to their advice and counsel.

2. Forgive your parents. Parents are human. Humans make mistakes. Parents make mistakes. In fact, the tough part about being a parent is that you know so little about it, and by the time you begin to get a handle on it, it's too late to make any difference. Your parents will make mistakes. Don't get angry and bitter at them. Learn to forgive them.

3. Obey your parents.

> Children, obey your parents in all things: for this is well pleasing unto the Lord.
>
> Colossians 3:20

> Children, obey your parents in the Lord: for this is right.
>
> Ephesians 6:1

Obedience is threefold. It is doing what I am told, when I am told to do it, and with the right heart attitude. Kids often obey along the first two dimensions but fail on the third. Like the little boy who was told to sit down and responded that he was sitting down on the outside but standing up on the inside, we often obey with the wrong attitude. This obedience is always exercised with a right heart attitude.

4. Respect your parents.

> Children, obey your parents in the Lord: for this is right.
>
> Ephesians 6:1

To honor your parents means to value or treasure them. Note the respect that Solomon had for his mother.

> Bath-sheba therefore went unto king Solomon to speak unto him for Adonijah. And the king rose up to meet her, and bowed himself unto her, and sat down on his throne, and caused a seat to be set for the king's mother; and she sat on his right hand.
>
> 1 Kings 2:19

Kids who are disrespectful to their parents create an atmosphere of hostility in the home.

5. ***Love your parents.*** Love is a gift and gifts are meant to be given. Tell your parents you love them. It may shock them, but they will be happy. I'm amazed at how many teenagers never tell their parents that they love them, and at how many parents never tell their kids they love them. Dr. Clyde Narramore has often reminded us that every member of the family ought to tell every other member of the family every day, "I love you."

6. ***Don't manipulate your parents.*** I have found that the manipulation of parents by children is one of the most serious problems in the home, created by the children themselves. Manipulation is playing one parent against the other. When Dad is easier on the children than Mom, then Mom feels like Dad never supports her authority and is constantly undermining her. When you play one parent against the other, you sow seeds of frustration, anger, and hostility between the parents.

7. ***Be understanding of your parents.*** Parents cannot afford to buy you everything you want. They work hard to pay the bills and often go through times of financial adversity. Be

understanding of your parents. Don't demand from them what they cannot give.

8. Love your brothers and sisters. Research indicates that one of the strongest emotional bonds is the one between brothers and sisters. Yet brothers and sisters seldom express that love to each other. Tell your brothers and sisters that you love them. Don't spend all your time arguing and fighting or demanding all the attention of your parents. Love your brothers and sisters.

9. Help your parents. Clean your room. Do the dishes. Set the table. Make your bed. Do it without being asked. You can make a positive contribution to your home by helping your parents. Recently my nine-year-old and five-year-old fixed breakfast on Saturday morning and brought it to the bedroom for my wife and me. Sugar cereal with no milk! I don't like that kind of cereal but I enjoyed every bite because it was an act of love.

10. Pray for your parents.

> I exhort therefore, that, first of all, supplications, prayers, intercessions, and giving of thanks, be made for all men;
>
> For kings, and for all that are in authority; that we may lead a quiet and peaceable life in all godliness and honesty.
>
> 1 Timothy 2:1,2

Pray for your parents. We believe that God hears and answers prayer and that He is capable of working miracles. Pray for your parents every day. Pray for your brothers and sisters. Pray for the needs of your family.

Conclusion

We see then that for the Christian home to work, every member must be involved, allowing God to direct individually in the lives of each one. Only then can God really enable the family to enter into the best that He desires for them. Remember, too, if you have really blown it up to now, and you wonder if God can ever put the pieces together, there is still hope. God specializes in the impossible. He loves to show His power in our weakness. You may be a long way from port. You're a long way from home. You will not undo years of wrong decisions overnight. But you can make one decision today. Decide that as for you and your house you will serve the Lord. Turn the ship around and at least be heading in the right direction. Commit yourself to building a godly home. That is one decision God is bound to bless and He will multiply it in the lives and hearts of all in your family.

Chapter Ten

Summary and Overview

Preaching is more than declaring the truth of Scripture. It is relating that truth to the everyday needs of human beings. John R. W. Stott, in his book entitled *Between Two Worlds,* argues that preaching is building a bridge between the world of biblical truth and the world of contemporary society. Stott argues that conservatives have a bent toward expanding and exegeting the truth but never apply it in a practical way to the lives and needs of people. They live and breathe in the world of the Bible, seldom relating it to the real world. On the other hand, liberal pastors begin in the real world and with psychological and sociological presuppositions attempt to address that world without dealing with biblical truth. Stott concludes that biblical preaching is building a bridge from the world of truth to the world of human need.

Building the Bridge

There are pastors in the local churches who labor faithfully to exegete the Word of God. They understand the etymology of the words, the tenses of the verbs, and the unique grammatical constructions. They pay attention to the context and the cultural implications of the text. They are experts in helping us understand the Bible but seldom help us apply its truth in a meaningful way. On the other hand, there are pastors who sound more like psychological cheerleaders than expositors of God's Word. Their messages are filled with real-life dramas, powerful quotes, and catchy sayings, but they seldom intersect with biblical truth.

The tension of these two worlds is clearly seen when one discusses the issue of marriage, divorce, and remarriage. For those who begin with sociological and humanistic presuppositions, their advice is obvious. "Try to stay married, but if it doesn't work out, don't worry. You can always divorce and remarry." For those who begin in the world of biblical interpretations with the presupposition that the Bible categorically prohibits divorce and remarriage, their advice is obvious. "You cannot divorce. You cannot remarry. If you have a legal divorce, you are still married in the eyes of God." This clear-cut rigidity makes it easy to apply one's interpretation to every situation. However, for those who, like me, believe that there are biblical grounds for divorce and remarriage, our advice in relating that truth to human situations is not as clear-cut and rigid. It is at this point where I confess my need for continual guidance and wisdom from God.

In this concluding chapter, I will identify the major biblical principles which we have discussed. I offer this overview in an attempt to build a biblical pattern out of which one can answer the specific needs of individuals and families. I admit that it is probably not a perfect structure but I offer it as a beginning point for those who want to address divorce and remarriage within the context of Scripture. I will give only the principle—I will not discuss it. It is important that you go back and review these principles as they are discussed in previous chapters.

The Principles of Marriage

Marriage is a covenant of companionship.
(Proverbs 2:17; Malachi 2:14).

God established guidelines when He brought Adam and Eve together (Genesis 1:26,27; 2:18–25):

1. God created male and female (1:26,27).
2. God recognized the need for companionship (2:18).
3. God gave certain requirements for marriage (vv. 24, 25): *separation, cleaving, becoming one flesh, shamelessness.*
4. God intended a permanent relationship (Matthew 19:4–6).

Husbands are to lead their homes and love their wives (Ephesians 5:21–32).

Wives are to submit to and reverence their husbands (vv. 21–32).

Parents are to train and nurture their children (6:1–3).

Children are to honor and obey their parents (vv. 1,2).

The Principles of Divorce

God intends permanence in the marriage relationship (Matthew 19:4–6; Romans 7:14; 1 Corinthians 7:39).

God permits divorce on the grounds of sexual immorality and of religious difference (when an unbeliever divorces a believer on the grounds of their faith in Christ) (Matthew 19:3–12; 1 Corinthians 7:10–28).

God permits remarriage to those who have a biblical basis for their divorce (Matthew 19:3–12; 1 Corinthians 7:10–28).

God desires reconciliation after separation and divorce (this is not always possible) (1 Corinthians 7:10,11).

The Principles of Remarriage

Remarriage is allowed only to those who have biblical grounds for their divorce (Matthew 19:3–12; 1 Corinthians 7:10–28).

Remarriage is allowed only when reconciliation is not feasible (1 Corinthians 7:10,11; 12–28).

Remarriage must be carefully and prayerfully pursued. The following questions should be answered before remarriage.

1. Is there a biblical basis for the divorce?
2. Is there hope for reconciliation?
3. Has there been time for spiritual and emotional healing?
4. Is the prospective spouse/date a committed Christian?
5. Does the new relationship emphasize mental, emotional, and spiritual intimacy and minimize physical intimacy?

The Principle of Forgiveness

God forgives those who have not lived by His principles. Those who are divorced and/or remarried without biblical grounds are* not *living in adultery if they have sought God's forgiveness. Those are decisions we cannot change. We must accept God's forgiveness, forget the past and live by God's principles in the present.

Conclusion

I hope you will not treat this book lightly. The issues related to marriage, divorce, and remarriage will not be solved by what I have written. I am convinced, however, that if you could gather the leading biblical scholars in the world and give them twelve months to develop one position on divorce, they could not do it. In fact, they would be no closer to unanimity after twelve months than they were the first day they met. I am still struggling with some of these issues. I do not have all the answers. However, I am thankful for the time I have spent studying the Scriptures. If you do nothing more than read and study the Scriptures mentioned in this book, then I will have accomplished my goal. If what I have said has helped, then I am grateful for the privilege. If you reject any or all of my conclusions, then I hope you will defend your position from the Scriptures.

Questions and Answers

It would be much easier to discuss the biblical principles related to marriage, divorce, and remarriage, and then leave the application of these principles to the reader. However, one of my primary concerns as a pastor is to relate truth to real-life situations. Consequently, I am including this section of *Questions and Answers.* These are questions drawn from real life. They are not hypothetical situations. I must confess that many of the questions are difficult and complex. I've tried to answer each one of them carefully, but I am aware of the danger that someone will twist what I say to his own advantage. Please read what I say with the understanding that I am not infallible and that many situations do *not* fit into a neat pattern which automatically delivers a simple answer. Please don't use me as an authority. "Well, Dobson says that . . ." If you agree or disagree with me, I hope that you will defend your position from the Word of God. This has been my only objective throughout this book. I want to get you back to the Bible and what *it* teaches on this important subject.

QUESTION: *My husband and I have been married for over ten years. His business takes him to another continent for six months at a* *time. When he is home, it is only for a month, and he is gone again. He is not born again. I was born again after we were married. Whenever I try to communicate or resolve conflict, he says I am fussing, and postpones discussion indefinitely. I don't feel married. I feel cheated. I don't feel comfortable with my married friends, and I don't fit into a singles group. I love the Lord and couldn't cope without Him. My question is, am I really married?*

ANSWER: Based on Genesis 2:24, since you experienced the following, you *are* married. As we have seen, marriage is a "covenant of companionship" (that is, an agreement where a man and woman commit to one another for life). Three elements characterize this commitment:

1. *Leaving*—you left your familial relationship to enter into one of a higher priority. You no longer allowed your parents to provide for you and exercise authority in your life. You separated yourself from them by the marriage covenant.

2. *Cleaving*—you became "glued together" and permanently bonded as a result of your personal commitment to one another.

3. *One flesh*—as your marriage was consummated you became united physically, mentally, and emotionally.

In addition, your marriage license and wedding band acknowledge before state and society this commitment.

Therefore, in the final analysis, the issue is not how you *feel*, but what you have done. This must be the starting point when approaching your legitimate problems. I would suggest that you seek pastoral counseling with your husband to work through the difficult problems which arise from your unique situation. In preparation for this, ask God to prepare your husband's heart to this end, as he does not seem very open to dealing with your concerns.

QUESTIONS ON REMARRIAGE TO FORMER SPOUSE: *A friend of mine divorced his wife because of adultery. She remarried, and now her second husband is dead. She wants to be reconciled to her first husband, and he and the kids are willing to do so. Since they are both Christians, is it all right?*

My ex-husband has remarried, and I have not. If his marriage ends through his present wife's death or through divorce, can I go back and remarry my ex-husband?

After twenty-five years of marriage, my husband left me to live with another woman. Prior to this, he had faithfully served the Lord. Because of childhood experiences, I had an aversion to sex, and my husband finally left me because of it. He eventually married the other woman, but he became convicted, returned to the church, and after a year, she divorced him. I now understand what my attitude towards sex should be. My friends at church and my children are praying and hoping my ex-husband and I will remarry. I am confused and very lonely. Is it permitted for us to remarry?

ANSWER: The question of remarrying a former spouse after a second marriage is one of the most frequently asked questions. In Deuteronomy 24:3,4, God states:

> And if the latter husband hate her, and write her a bill of divorcement, and giveth it in her hand, and sendeth her out of his house; or if the latter husband die, which took her to be his wife;
>
> Her former husband, which sent her away, may not take her again to be his wife, after that she is defiled; for that is abomination before the Lord: and thou shalt not cause the land to sin, which the Lord thy God giveth thee for an inheritance.

These verses indicate that after a second marriage a person may not return to their first partner. To do so is "an abomination before the Lord." Why? I think the principle communicated in this passage is that God does not want the issue of divorce and remarriage to be reduced to wife-swapping with little or no commitment to the covenant of marriage.

Does that mean that in the twentieth century returning to one's original partner after a second marriage is still prohibited? God sheds further light on this issue in Jeremiah 3:1.

> They say, If a man put away his wife, and she go from him, and become another man's, shall he return unto her again? shall not that land be greatly polluted? but thou hast played the harlot with many lovers; yet return again to me, saith the Lord.
>
> Jeremiah 3:1

In Jeremiah God compares His relationship with Israel to that of a couple who have been divorced. According to the Mosaic Law, after the divorce, the wife could not return to her original husband after she had married another. Even though Israel was in that same position, God invites her to "return again to me." It seems to me that this is an exception to the prohibition of Deuteronomy 24. Consequently, in certain circumstances, it may be permissible to return to the original partner after a second marriage.

Now let me respond specifically to the questions. I think you ought to carefully consider whether or not you should return to your original partner. If after much prayer and counsel you make that decision, I do not think you are violating the Scripture. One person wrote the following:

> My wife and I married during World War I, but during the Depression I backslid and lived immorally and she divorced me. We both remarried. Her husband is deceased. After my second wife died, I rededicated my life to God. Five years ago, my first wife and I remarried. We are very happy and depend on each other very much.

I think that what these people did does *not* contradict the principles of God's Word.

QUESTION: *How can a murderer or child molester, and so forth, repent, be forgiven, and become a pastor or deacon, but not a divorced person?*

ANSWER: The Bible is clear that when a man is forgiven by God he is cleansed of all his past (1 John 1:9). This includes murder, child molestation, or divorce. To say a person cannot serve in an office of the church does not say they have not been forgiven or that they can in no way serve God. However, we must acknowledge the explicit qualifications for pastor and deacons given by Paul in 1 Timothy 3. The pastor or deacon is to be the "husband of one wife" (vv. 2,12) and in my opinion, this would exclude those who have been divorced. Further, another explicit qualification is that a pastor or deacon must rule their own household well (vv. 4,12). The word Paul uses for *rule* literally means "manage." There can be no doubt that divorce is the result of the ultimate mismanagement of one's household. Therefore, God has put the no-divorce requirement on the offices of pastor and deacon, and we have an obligation to accept this as legitimate.

Furthermore, it is improbable that God would call a former rapist, murderer, or child molester to the office of pastor and deacon in light of the qualification that they be "blameless" (vv. 2, 10).

QUESTION: *If it is a sin for one Christian to take another to court, does this not make divorce a sin for Christians?*

ANSWER: The Bible clearly states that believers are to solve their legal disputes within the confines and authority of the church.

> Dare any of you, having a matter against another, go to law before the unjust, and not before the saints?

> Do ye not know that the saints shall judge the world? and if the world shall be judged by you, are ye unworthy to judge the smallest matters?
>
> Know ye not that we shall judge angels? how much more things that pertain to this life?
>
> If then ye have judgments of things pertaining to this life, set them to judge who are least esteemed in the church.
>
> If I speak to your shame. Is it so, that there is not a wise man among you? no, not one that shall be able to judge between his brethren?
>
> But brother goeth to law with brother, and that before the unbelievers.
>
> Now therefore there is utterly a fault among you, because ye go to law one with another. Why do ye not rather take wrong? Why do ye not rather suffer yourselves to be defrauded?
>
> Nay, ye do wrong, and defraud, and that your brethren.
>
> 1 Corinthians 6:1–8

As a pastor I have been involved in arbitrating legal disputes between Christians. This is an important function of the local assembly.

How does this prohibition against going to court against another brother relate to divorce? Since a divorce necessitates legal procedures before a secular court, does this mean that Christians who secure such a divorce are sinning against God by violating 1 Corinthians 6:1–8? First, I believe the church should intercede and attempt to prevent the divorce from taking place (see chapter 6, Divorce and the Church).

Second, while marriage involves responsibility to God, in our society it involves the sanction of civil authority. A pastor who performs a marriage does it with the sanction and approval of the state. The state also mandates requirements for dissolving that marriage. Believers who seek to marry must conform to the laws of the land and likewise those who seek divorce must conform to the laws which govern that divorce. Caesar has exercised authority over marriage and divorce and as Christians we have an obligation to conform to those laws. Getting a divorce through the court is no more a violation of 1 Corinthians 6 than getting a marriage license. Neither violates this passage.

> Let every soul be subject unto the higher powers. For there is no power but of God: the powers that be are ordained of God.
>
> Romans 13:1

I do not think that going to court for a divorce is a violation of 1 Corinthians 6.

QUESTION: *As a single, Christian college student, I am deeply disturbed by books on the "will of God," which suggest that God is not involved in the details of my life, and that I have to make all my own decisions. Is there really not someone in particular God wants me to marry?*

ANSWER: At the root of this question is the more basic and controversial question: Does God have a will for my life, and can I discover it? Two extreme views have been offered in answer to this question. One view suggests that God has an individual will for each person, and that it is man's responsibility to determine God's will for every detail, no matter how petty. The other view asserts that God does not have a particular will for each individual, outside of certain moral standards, and man's responsibility is simply to exercise wisdom within this freedom, and whatever he chooses becomes God's will for him.

A balanced view recognizes that God does indeed have a particular will for every individual, but that will does not extend to the trivial and mundane, but is directed toward life-affecting decisions. This is evidenced in the life of Paul as six times he states he is an apostle, which is a life-affecting vocation, "by the will of God." As marriage is undoubtedly a life-affecting decision, God certainly has a particular time and person in mind for the Christian. This is biblically supported in the example of God's involvement in the selection of a wife for Isaac when Abraham's servant testified, ". . . I being in the way, *the Lord led* me to the house of my master's brethren (Genesis 24:27, italics added). By God's working to bring a particular woman in contact with Abraham's servant in response to prayer, this illustrates the specific nature of God's will and justifies our confidence that He will do the same for us if asked. Further substantiation is found in the fact that God is our Father, and desires to provide ". . . good things to them who ask him" (Matthew 7:11). Earthly fathers provide direction for their children as needed. So, likewise, our heavenly Father will provide direction as His children need it.

QUESTION: *My first husband cheated on me and then divorced me. My second husband was painfully hard to live with, but I honored my commitment to him. He recently passed away, and I am thinking about remarriage. My prospective husband is also divorced, and I am wondering would God honor this marriage?*

ANSWER: Because your first marriage was dissolved on scriptural grounds in that your husband committed adultery (Matthew 19:9), and your second husband died, which also scripturally dissolves marital bonds, there is no problem for you to remarry. The question involves whether *your prospective husband is free to remarry scripturally.* He is free IF his first marriage ended as a result of infidelity (19:9) or desertion as described in 1 Corinthians 7:12–15. Further, Paul requires in 2 Corinthians 6:14 that a believer only marry another believer so as not to be "unequally yoked."

This proposed marriage is therefore biblically acceptable as long as your prospective husband is a believer and was scripturally divorced. Yes, God could honor this marriage.

QUESTION: *If someone marries a divorced person, can that person ever be forgiven for living in adultery as long as they are married? Further, if you continue in such a relationship, this reveals you are not sorry, so how can you be forgiven?*

ANSWER: As the biblical record of David and Bathsheba reveals, by the fact that there was no requirement given by God through the prophet Nathan to dissolve the relationship (2 Samuel 12:11–15), it is not God's desire that the marriage be dissolved by divorce, even though it was begun in adultery. Once forgiveness is obtained and the sin removed (2 Samuel 12:13), though there may still be lingering consequences, further repentance in reference to the initial adulterous behavior is not required. There is no constant state of adultery. To say that it is constant would make divorce the unpardonable sin, which it is not (Matthew 12:31). Therefore, someone who willfully violates Scripture to divorce and remarry can repent and seek the forgiveness of God, and thereby be restored into the fellowship of the church. I think God meets us at our point of need, forgives us, and builds our lives from that point on. It is impossible to go back and change the bad decisions of the past.

QUESTION: *Is it proper for a pastor to marry two previously divorced Christians?*

ANSWER: Possibly, if the previous divorces of both parties were on scriptural grounds. This would be the case if both marriages were dissolved on the basis of desertion (1 Corinthians 7:15) or infidelity (Matthew 19:9). And, if it were the case that one or both of the parties desiring to be married were the perpetrators of the divorce, repentance must take place. If these qualifications are not met, the pastor should not marry them as this would promote adultery (Matthew 19:9), or fail to deal with unrepented sin. Premarital counseling is always in order (as there may be unresolved problems), and the pastor should consider each case on its own merits.

QUESTION: *If divorce is okay once, what if the second marriage doesn't work?*

ANSWER: God hates divorce (Malachi 2:16) and in a sense it is never okay. However, in spite of the fact that divorce is never desirable in God's eyes, it is acceptable after all efforts are made to reconcile and the scriptural guidelines are met. There is no biblical limit to the number of divorces that can be justifiably pursued. It is conceivable a person could marry an unfaithful individual more than once. However, common sense would suggest that if you are involved in a second divorce, most likely you are not taking the marriage commitment seriously enough, or you are not exercising God's wisdom in selecting a mate or in managing the home. I would suggest that you seek pastoral counseling to deal with potentially unresolved problems which will continue to disrupt your home.

QUESTION: *Do principles regarding pastors and deacons carry over to board members or lay directors of a retreat ministry?*

ANSWER: Yes, if the retreat ministry serves as an arm of a local church and if by function the board members or lay directors are equated with deacons or pastors. This can best be determined by the local church in question. We must caution against not upholding the qualifications of those who serve as pastors and deacons under another name. Perhaps the retreat ministry in question is not an arm of a local church ministry, but is instead an independent parachurch organization. The general principle that God requires more of leadership should be applied as demonstrated by legislated matters regarding the spiritual leaders of Israel (Leviticus 21:7; 18–20). Therefore it would be wise to avoid having divorcées taking leadership roles.

QUESTION: *Why struggle to keep a marriage together when others divorce and remarry, and as Christians come under no church* *discipline and serve in other leadership positions besides pastor or deacon?*

ANSWER: First, we must always "struggle" to keep a marriage together because when God joins a couple together, He desires they stay together (Matthew 19:6). And, our chief desire must be to please God regardless of what others may do. Further, "Be not deceived God is not mocked. . ." (Galatians 6:7), for God will implement the necessary discipline and chastening even if the church does not. Second, your question points out the need for all ministries to be under the umbrella of the local church and for every Christian to be subject to effective local church discipline. Sadly today many churches do not exercise discipline of members, but this does not entitle us to "give up" on our marriage nor does it justify the placement of divorced men who have not repented in leadership positions.

QUESTION: *If the chain of command is God, then man, then woman, may we conclude that a man may divorce his wife, but that a woman may not divorce her husband?*

ANSWER: No. First, let us assert that in Christ, God does not acknowledge a different standard for male and female (Galatians 3:28). Second, this principle is upheld in Paul's discourse regarding desertion (1 Corinthians 7:12–15) where he addresses both sexes equally. Third, because Mark 10:12 acknowledges divorce from both the perspective of the male and female, when this is harmonized with Matthew 19:9, both sexes are under the same standard.

QUESTION: *Is lust the same as adultery? And if so, can a person have grounds for divorce if the spouse is continually lusting?*

ANSWER: Yes, lust is the same as adultery in that it equally violates God's standard of moral purity (Matthew 5:27,28). However, it is not the same in *consequence.* To think an act in no way makes one subject to the same discipline as one who *committed* the act. Thus, in no way can Scripture be construed to allow divorce on the grounds of lust. Further, in practice it would be impossible to accommodate all those who could file for divorce on these grounds. It would make a mockery of the true nature of marriage.

QUESTION: *My husband asked me for a divorce so he could marry another woman. I gave him one and knew it was wrong. I never dated afterward, but prayed for my ex-husband to return. After nine years he did. We are now remarried, and I am happy. Did I sin by remarrying him?*

ANSWER: No, you did not. The case of Hosea and his unconditional love for Gomer has been demonstrated in your life. Jeremiah 3:1 suggests it is permissible to go back to the original partner after a second marriage (see the questions and answers at the beginning of this section which relate to this issue in light of Deuteronomy 24).

QUESTION: *My son married at age twenty and divorced after four months. His ex-wife is now married and has a child. He is now thirty years old, and dating a fine Christian girl. Is he free to remarry?*

ANSWER: First, the amount of time elapsed and the fact that a child has been born is irrelevant. The son is free to remarry in any case due to the fact that his wife remarried, which dissolved the initial union. If applicable, the son must repent if the dissolving of the first relationship was a result of his desertion (1 Corinthians 7:15) or infidelity (Matthew 19:9), in order to ensure the potential for God's blessing on this proposed union.

QUESTION: *I married at age 15 and left my husband to run around with other men. My husband married again, but his wife left* *him. I have since become a Christian. I don't want to go back to my husband, but want to marry a Christian. It was my fault we separated, so can I get married again and still please God?*

ANSWER: First, the remarriage of your first husband dissolved your marital bond with him as well as your adulterous behavior (Matthew 19:9). Second, when you became a Christian you were made a "new" creature (2 Corinthians 5:17), and all your sin was forgiven (1 John 1:9). Therefore, you are free to remarry as long as your spouse is scripturally qualified in that he is a believer (2 Corinthians 6:14) and if divorced, is also scripturally qualified.

QUESTION: *My husband and I both had been previously divorced. We both brought children into our marriage and then had a son together. Though we are Christians, my husband became violent and left me, and now we are divorced. We both still attend the same church, but he is seeing someone else. Should I pray for reconciliation? (Note: He does not communicate or come to see his son, and there was no adultery while we were married.)*

ANSWER: As your divorce did not involve adultery, unless your husband has since committed adultery, the essential bond of union still exists and therefore you should pray for reconciliation as your divorce was not scriptural (Matthew 19:9). If he has committed adultery since your divorce was finalized, you may continue to pray for reconciliation if you wish to, but scripturally you are free to remarry. My advice is to continue to pray for reconciliation.

QUESTION: *My first husband was guilty of adultery and perhaps homosexuality so I know our divorce was biblical. I met a man who did not try to take advantage of me as others did, and we became emotionally involved. He has since built a house for me. The problem is his wife never gave him a divorce, and she lives across the country.*

However, he provides a separate household for us, I use his last name, and he promises to marry me when his wife dies. Would this be biblical? Should I leave him? I want God's will.

ANSWER: Biblically there is no justification for maintaining your present situation. The man with whom you are currently involved is still legally and morally bound to his wife. Until that marriage is scripturally dissolved, you are obligated to discontinue the relationship, and as a practical step you should totally disassociate yourself from him (i.e., move out of the house, etc.). Based on what you told us, he has no reason to seek a divorce from his present wife. Your involvement with him is only an invitation for him to commit sin. You should seek good Christian fellowship, until such time as God will bring someone into your life who is scripturally qualified to be your mate. In fact, your continued relationship with him may prohibit a reconciliation with his wife which is what God desires.

QUESTION: *My ex-wife committed adultery, and I divorced her. My present wife divorced her first husband before she was saved. When we got married, we thought it was all right biblically. Now we are not sure, so we are separated. We love each other and do not want to divorce. Are we living in sin? Should we divorce or can we continue in this marriage and serve God?*

ANSWER: Your first marriage was dissolved on scriptural grounds. If there is a problem, it would be with your wife's divorce. Unless her first marriage was dissolved on the basis of adultery (Matthew 19:9), or desertion (1 Corinthians 7:15), your wife is still technically bound to her first husband and would be considered adulterous, as you also would be (Matthew 5:32). In light of the fact that you have remarried, and in light of the tremendous complexity which would result from dissolving your current relationship, your wife needs to repent of her wrong and seek a God-honoring relationship with you. On the other hand, if her previous marriage was scripturally dissolved you are not living in sin, and you can certainly continue in this marriage and serve God. I think you must seek God's forgiveness and ask Him to help to make your current marriage one that is stable and honors Him.

QUESTION: *Our new pastor thinks it is okay to have divorced deacons. Our church has never believed this previously, and we are concerned about the impression it would leave on the young people by voting in divorced deacons. How would you perceive the future of such a church? Would this blunt the church's spirituality?*

ANSWER: As any violation of God's Word would inhibit spiritual growth, so this violation of 1 Timothy 3:12 will also. This is not to say that the church cannot grow, but there is no doubt that growth would be limited, as everything rises and falls on leadership. God requires blamelessness in those who would challenge others to be holy even as God is holy (1 Peter 1:15,16).

QUESTION: *It's easier to be a widow than to be a divorcée because a widow is respected and pitied, while a divorcée is judged and condemned, even at church. Why do happily married men always teach on the subject of divorce? How can they understand what it's like? I think pastors need to be more understanding and sympathetic.*

ANSWER: In no way is the church justified in not respecting those who have suffered a scriptural divorce, or who have received God's forgiveness for failing in their marriage. The divorced person is not to be considered a second-class citizen in the church, even though such a person may not serve as pastor or deacon as stipulated in 1 Timothy 3:2, 12. The church must acknowledge what God has acknowledged in the forgiveness of the divorce (1 John 1:9). One does not have to suffer the emotional hurts and consequences of sin in order to accurately teach from God's Word on this subject. However, there is no scriptural reason why a divorcee could not teach scriptural principles regarding marriage, divorce, and remarriage, and perhaps more should.

QUESTION: *I was scripturally divorced and remarried. A year ago I was ordained and became a deacon, believing it was God's will; I even thought perhaps God was calling me to preach. What should I do?*

ANSWER: Based on 1 Timothy 3:2 and 12, I believe that divorced people are excluded from the office of deacon or pastor. Therefore, you should resign your position and look for alternative ways to serve God in your local church. However, good people disagree with my interpretation, and you will have to decide what you think the Bible teaches.

QUESTION: *Should a divorced person be married by a pastor or a Justice of the Peace?*

ANSWER: A divorced person ought to first determine if he or she is qualified for remarriage, and should seek the assistance of a trained pastor in doing this. If it can be biblically demonstrated that a divorced person is free to remarry, then it would be best to marry upon the authority of the church and the pastor before God and His people.

QUESTION: *My wife left me three years ago, and I have two young sons. I don't believe in divorce, but I met a young lady who loves my boys, and they love her. I don't know where my wife is, and she has never contacted us. Would it be all right to divorce my wife and marry again?*

ANSWER: First of all, let us establish that unless there were scriptural grounds for divorce from your wife, you are not free to divorce her until you have sought to be reconciled. If reconciliation is impossible, due to your inability to contact your wife, then it is justifiable to dissolve the marriage on the grounds of desertion (1 Corinthians 7:12–15). Upon the dissolution of your marriage on scriptural grounds, you would then be free to remarry.

QUESTION: *If marriage is a spiritual bond, how can divorce break it?*

ANSWER: First of all, let us clarify that the biblical concept of "one flesh" involves more than the spiritual dimension, but includes a "oneness" of mind, emotions, will, and physical being. Therefore, legal divorce does not break the bond. However, *porneia* does (Matthew 19:9), as does desertion (1 Corinthians 7:15). The Old Testament establishes that *porneia* broke this bond in that violators were stoned to death. Divorce was an act of God's grace to allow for the sustaining of the adulterer's life, while allowing the innocent party to view the former relationship as truly broken and the former spouse as dead (Deuteronomy 22:22–24). In a similar way, divorce on the grounds of desertion allows freedom from the former union (1 Corinthians 7:15). The basic principle is that the marriage bond is broken by death. In the Law of Moses this death principle was extended to encompass the one who committed adultery, and Paul extended it to the one who deserted his spouse. This allows the innocent party to carry on with life, as though the former partner were dead.

QUESTION: *If a man puts his wife away and she remarries an innocent party, is he causing her to commit adultery?*

ANSWER: Based on Matthew 5:32, it is clear that the husband who unscripturally divorces his wife does indeed cause her to commit adultery. Further, the man who decides to marry such a woman also commits adultery (Luke 16:18). The apparent reason for this is because she is technically still bound to her first husband because the essential bond of unity was not broken by means of *porneia* (Matthew 5:32, 19:9), or desertion

(1 Corinthians 7:15). From God's perspective, since the original union is not broken, the second marriage is seen the same as an adulterous affair.

QUESTION: *How do you resolve the dilemma between the Old Testament Law and the New Testament, when the Old Testament permitted polygamy?*

ANSWER: Did the Old Testament really permit polygamy or simply tolerate it without applying specific acts of divine judgment to end its practice? It would appear that God nowhere states He permits polygamy and simply allows the natural consequence of this wrongful act to serve as indication that He had not designed marriage this way. In every biblical case of polygamy, no small amount of family upheaval and disruption resulted from these ill-advised multiple unions. God's intention is indicated in the first family He created: Adam and Eve. The pattern is one man for one woman for one lifetime. God never at any time indicates that He will sanction or bless anything outside of this pattern. It is true that the Old Testament does not make strong statements against polygamy. Neither does it support it. Every polygamous marriage given in the Old Testament had significant problems. First Corinthians 10:11 tells us that the experiences of the saints in the Old Testament who lived this type of life-style should serve as a negative example, warning us of the results of exceeding the God-ordained pattern for marriage.

QUESTION: *When Jesus said that if a man put away his wife for a reason other than for fornication, that man caused his wife to commit adultery, could it not mean that if a man divorced an innocent wife, and she remarried, then he is responsible for her committing adultery?*

ANSWER: Yes, based on the voice and meaning of the word *cause* (Greek-*poieo*), the Scriptures do declare the husband to be responsible for the wife's adultery should he wrongfully divorce her. This can certainly be applied generically, if a wife wrongfully divorces her husband and he remarries, she is responsible for his adultery should he remarry. The active voice of the verb *poieo* tells us the husband is not to be considered passive but actively responsible for the result of his wrongful divorce. Further, a revealing insight into the meaning of the verb "cause" is seen in Mark 7:37 where the identical Greek construction is used. In reference to Jesus it says, ". . . he *maketh* both the deaf to hear, and the dumb to speak" (italics added). Jesus *made* them do something they could not do on their own. Jesus alone bore the responsibility for their hearing and sight. No credit could go to them. In like manner, the spouse who unjustly puts away his or her mate bears their responsibility for the adultery that results from that mate's remarriage. However, the primary responsibility must be accepted by the person who *commits* the act of adultery.

QUESTION: *I am concerned that in our efforts to love and help divorced people that we may condone sin. If the innocent party remarries and therefore becomes guilty of adultery, how are we to view God's attitude toward such a marriage?*

ANSWER: God is not pleased with the remarriage of an innocent party who has been wrongfully divorced. How do we know? Because Luke 16:18 makes it clear that the second husband becomes an adulterer by marrying her, and surely God would not be pleased with a marriage which results in adultery. Where does that leave the innocent party? Until the bond of marriage with the first spouse is broken through death or *porneia,* there is an opportunity and obligation for reconciliation. However, if the person repents and seeks God's forgiveness, he can experience God's blessing. I do not think that one can go back and undo the consequences of sinful decision making. We must accept God's forgiveness and go on from there.

QUESTION: *You said the word* unclean *in the Old Testament meant "shameful conduct associated with sexual activity." Could you be more specific? Also, you said a New Testament definition of* fornication *was sexual perversion. Exactly what does that mean?*

ANSWER: The Hebrew word for *uncleanness* ('ervah) literally means "nakedness of a thing," thus implying some sort of shameful physical exposure. Most likely, this indecency resulted from illicit sexual conduct, short of adultery. This would seem logical in light of the fact that the Mosaic Law proscribed the death penalty for those who committed adultery, and a person who wanted to pursue illicit sexual intimacy would naturally want to avoid such harsh consequences. As to specific parameters of behavior encompassed in this word's meaning, we cannot say. It may refer to the exposure and fondling of another person's body, which do not technically constitute the conjugal act but are nevertheless associated with sexual activity (*see* Proverbs 5:15–19; Song of Solomon 5:10–16; 7:1–10).

Porneia is a broad term which should be understood to refer to illicit sexual intercourse in general. This can be demonstrated, as *porneia* is used throughout the New Testament to refer to various types of sexual perversion, that is, anything that varies from the God-ordained ideal. For instance, in 1 Corinthians 5:1, Paul uses *porneia* in reference to an incestuous and adulterous relationship. Further, in Jude 7, *porneia* is used in reference to the sin of Sodom and Gomorrah. Genesis 19 indicates that this sin was that of homosexuality. Paul also used *porneia* to refer to premarital sex in 1 Corinthians 7:1,2. Therefore, *porneia* should be understood as *any sexual sin.*

QUESTION: *Is divorce acceptable for severe mental and physical abuse?*

ANSWER: This is perhaps one of the most difficult questions to answer. My heart tells me that a wife who has been physically and emotionally abused should have every right to divorce her husband. Let me set aside my heart for a moment, and address this question from the Bible. Some pastors suggest that because a woman should be in submission to her husband, she is obligated to stay with him no matter what the situation. This is ridiculous advice. If a woman is being physically abused and the welfare and emotional well-being of the children are in jeopardy, she ought to leave her husband immediately. She should find protection from family or friends, at a home for battered women, or within the church. She should not return to her husband until he has undergone professional counseling, and she is confident that the abuse will not recur. Does she have the right to divorce her husband? The Bible does not speak to this particular situation. There are no biblical grounds for divorce that include wife abuse. To permit divorce on these grounds would be to allow what the Bible does not. However, the battered wife has every right to remain separated from her husband for her own protection and for the protection of the children.

QUESTION: *My husband is presently having an affair and has filed for a divorce. I love him and do not want a divorce. If this divorce becomes final does that mean that God is telling me that it was not meant for us to stay together? Will my husband be the one to answer to God for the dissolving of this marriage? How about his girlfriend? Further, when he comes home to see our baby daughter, how should I act toward him? Should I be like Hosea in the Bible?*

ANSWER: Your love for your husband is commendable and certainly God would desire your following the example of Hosea in continuing to exercise such undeserved love. However, God recognizes that the hardness of men's hearts (Matthew 19:8) does not always allow for the maintaining of the marital bond, because greater personal destruction often results. Therefore, a finalized divorce does not mean God never meant for you to stay together, but rather that He permitted divorce because of the hardness of your husband's heart. I would suggest you prayerfully consider whether divorce may be the more appropriate action for you should your husband refuse to repent and reconcile. Based on Matthew 5:32 and 19:9, it is clear your husband will be held accountable for the divorce as he, not you, committed sin. In Old Testament days your husband and his mistress would have been stoned for their adulterous behavior and you would not. This clearly shows with whom God places the responsibility for breaking up your home.

In reference to your behavior when he comes to visit your baby girl, it is always demanded that as a Christian, you act Christian. This involves demonstrating Christlike kindness and courtesy. However, this does not give him a right to mistreat you or take advantage of you. This is a difficult line to draw and I would suggest you pray for the wisdom to know the difference.

Bibliography and Further Reading

Adams, Jay E. *Marriage, Divorce and Remarriage.* Phillipsburg, New Jersey: Presbyterian and Reformed Publishing Co., 1981.

———. *Marriage, Divorce and Remarriage in the Bible.* Phillipsburg, New Jersey: Presbyterian and Reformed Publishing Co., 1981.

Ames, L. "Children and Divorce: What the Teacher Can Do." *Educational Digest,* November 1969, pp. 19–21.

Atkinson, David. *To Have and to Hold: The Marriage Covenant and the Discipline of Divorce.* London: Collins, 1979.

Bane, Mary Jo. "Marital Disruption and the Lives of Children." *Journal of the Social Issues,* 1976, Vol. 32, pp. 103–116.

Barber, Cyril J. "What is Marriage?" *Journal of Psychology and Theology* 2(1974):48–60.

Bartling, Walter J. "Sexuality, Marriage, and Divorce in 1 Corinthians 6:12–7:16–A Practical Exercise in Hermeneutics." *Concordia Theological Monthly* 29 (1968):255–66.

Boice, James Montgomery. "The Biblical View of Divorce." *Eternity,* December 1970, pp. 19–21.

Bontrager, G. Edwin. *Divorce and the Faithful Church.* Scottdale, Pennsylvania: Herald Press, 1978.

Bromiley, Geoffrey W. *God and Marriage.* Grand Rapids, Michigan: Wm. B. Eerdmans Publishing Co., 1980.

Brown, Bob W. *Getting Married Again.* Waco, Texas: Word, Inc., 1979.

Bustanoby, Andre. *You Can Change Your Personality.* Grand Rapids, Michigan: Zondervan, 1976.

Carroll, Anne Kristin. *From the Brink of Divorce.* Garden City, New York: Doubleday, Galilee, 1978.

Chapman, Gary D. *Hope for the Separated.* Chicago, Illinois: Moody Press, 1982.

———. *Toward a Growing Marriage.* Chicago, Illinois: Moody, 1979.

Coiner, H. G. "Those 'Divorce and Remarriage' Passages (Matt. 5:32; 19:9; 1 Cor. 7:10–16)." *Concordia Theological Monthly* 39(June 1968), pp. 367–84.

Crook, Roger H. *An Open Book to the Christian Divorcee.* Nashville, Tennessee: Broadman, 1974.

Dahl, Gerald L. *Why Christian Marriages Are Breaking Up.* Nashville, Tennessee: Thomas Nelson, 1979.

DeHaan, Richard W. *Marriage, Divorce, and Remarriage.* Grand Rapids, Michigan: Radio Bible Class, 1979.

Duty, Guy. *Divorce and Remarriage.* Minneapolis, Minnesota: Bethany Fellowship, 1967.

Eichhorst, William R. "Ezra's Ethics on Intermarriage and Divorce." *Grace Journal* 10:3(Fall 1969):16–28.

Ellison, Stanley A. *Divorce and Remarriage in the Church.* Grand Rapids, Michigan: Zondervan, 1977.

Evans, William. *The Right and Wrong in Divorce and Remarriage.* Grand Rapids, Michigan: Zondervan, 1946.

Fine, M. A., Moreland, J. R., and Schwebel, A. I. "Long-Term Effects of Divorce on Parent-Child Relationships." *Developmental Psychology,* 1983, Vol. 19, No. 5, pp. 703–13.

Fisher-Hunter, W. *Marriage and Divorce.* Waynesboro, Pennsylvania: MacNeish Publishers, 1952.

Francke, L. and Reese, M. "The Child of Divorce." *Newsweek,* February 11, 1980, pp. 58–60.

Furstenberg, F. F. Jr., Peterson, J. L., Nord, C. W., and Zill, N.

"The Life Course of Children of Divorce: Marital Disruption and Parental Contact." *American Sociological Review,* 1983, Vol. 48, pp. 656–68.

Glassock, Ed, "The 'Husband of One Wife' Requirement in I Timothy 3.2." *Bibliotheca Sacra* 140 (1983):244–58.

Grollman, Earl A., ed. *Explaining Divorce to Children.* Boston, Massachusetts: Beacon Press, 1969.

Hensley, J. Clark. *Coping With Being Single Again.* Nashville, Tennessee: Broadman, 1978.

Heth, William A. "Another Look at the Erasmian View of Divorce and Remarriage." *Journal of the Evangelical Theological Society* 25 (1982):263–72.

——— and Wenham, Gordon J. *Jesus and Divorce.* Nashville, Tennessee: Thomas Nelson, 1985.

Hocking, David. *Marrying Again.* Old Tappan, New Jersey: Fleming H. Revell, 1983.

Johnson, James. *Loneliness is Not Forever.* Chicago, Illinois: Moody, 1979.

Kalter, N. and Rembar, J. "The Significance of a Child's Age at the Time of Parental Divorce." *American Journal of Orthopsychiatry* 51 (1981):85–100.

Kellam, S. G., Ensminger, M. E., Turner, R. J. "Family Structure and the Mental Health of Children." *Arch General Psychiatry.* 34, September 1977, pp. 1012–23.

Laney, J. Carl. *The Divorce Myth.* Minneapolis, Minnesota: Bethany House Publishers, 1981.

MacKinnon, C. E., Brody, G. H., and Stoneman, Z. "The Effects of Divorce and Maternal Employment on the Home Environments of Preschool Children." *Child Development,* 1982, 53, pp. 1392–99.

McGinnis, Alan Loy. *The Friendship Factor: How to Get Closer to the People You Care For.* Minneapolis, Minnesota: Augsburg, 1979.

Martin, John R. *Divorce and Remarriage: A Perspective for Counseling.* Scottdale, Pennsylvania: Herald Press, 1974.

Meier, Paul D. *You Can Avoid Divorce.* Grand Rapids, Michigan: Baker Book House, 1978.

Miles, Herbert J. *Sexual Happiness in Marriage.* Grand Rapids, Michigan: Zondervan, 1982.

———. *Sexual Understanding Before Marriage.* Grand Rapids, Michigan: Zondervan, 1972.

Montefiore, H. "Jesus on Divorce and Remarriage." In *Marriage, Divorce and the Church,* pp. 79–95. London: SPCK, 1971.

Murray, John. *Divorce.* Phillipsburg, New Jersey: Presbyterian and Reformed Publishing Co., 1961.

Narramore, S. Bruce. *Adolescence Is Not An Illness.* Old Tappan, New Jersey: Fleming H. Revell, 1980.

Peters, George W. *Divorce and Remarriage.* Chicago, Illinois: Moody, 1970.

Phillips, C. *Our Family Got a Divorce.* Glendale, California: Regal Books, 1979.

Plekker, Robert J. *Divorce and the Christian.* Wheaton, Illinois: Tyndale House Publishers, 1980.

Ryrie, Charles C. "Biblical Teaching on Divorce and Remarriage." *Grace Theological Journal* 3 (1982):177–92.

———. *The Role of Women in the Church.* Chicago, Illinois: Moody, 1979.

Santrock, John W. "Paternal Absence, Sex Typing, and Identification." *Developmental Psychology,* 1970, Vol. 2, No. 2, pp. 264–272.

———. "Relation of Type and Onset of Father Absence to Cognitive Development." *Child Development,* 1972, 43, pp. 455–69.

Saucy, Robert L. "The Husband of One Wife." *Bibliotheca Sacra* 131 (July-September, 1974), pp. 229–40.

Shaner, Donald W. *A Christian View of Divorce According to the Teachings of the New Testament.* Leiden: E. J. Brill, 1969.

Shinn, Marybeth, "Father Absence and Children's Cognitive Development." *Psychological Bulletin,* 1978, Vol. 85, No. 2, pp. 295–324.

Small, Dwight Hervey. Review of *Marriage, Divorce and Remarriage in the Bible,* by Jay E. Adams. *Eternity,* June 1981, pp. 44–5.

———. *The Right to Remarry.* Old Tappan, New Jersey: Fleming H. Revell, 1975.

Smith, Virginia Watts. *The Single Parent,* Old Tappan, N.J.: Fleming H. Revell, 1976, 1983.

Smoke, Jim. *Growing Through Divorce.* Irvine, California: Harvest House, 1976.

Steele, Paul E., and Ryrie, Charles C. *Meant to Last.* Wheaton, Illinois: SP Publications, 1983.

Stott, J.R.W. "The Biblical Teaching on Divorce." *Churchman* 85 (1971):165–74.

Suarez, J. M., Weston, N. L., Hartstein, N. B. "Mental Health Interventions in Divorce Proceedings." *American Journal of Orthopsychiatry.* 48 (2), April 1978, pp. 273–83.

Swihart, Judson J. and Brigham, Steven L. *Helping Children of Divorce.* Downers Grove, Illinois: Inter-Varsity Press, 1982.

Swihart, Judson J. *How Do You Say, "I Love You"?* Downers Grove, Illinois: Inter-Varsity Press, 1977.

Swihart, P. *How to Live With Your Feelings.* Downers Grove, Illinois: Inter-Varsity Press, 1976.

Swindoll, Charles R. *Divorce: When It All Comes Tumbling Down.* Portland, Oregon: Multnomah Press, 1981.

———. *Strike the Original Match.* Portland, Oregon: Multnomah Press, 1980.

Tessman, Lora. *Children of Parting Parents.* New York: Jason Aronson, 1978.

Visher, E., and Visher, J. *Step Families.* New York: Brenner/Mazel, 1979.

Wallerstein, J. S. and Kelly, J. B. "Children and Divorce: A Review." *Social Work,* November 1979, pp. 468–75.

———. "Effects of Parental Divorce: The Adolescent Experience." In *The Child in His Family,* ed. E. James Anthony and Cyrill Koupernik. New York: John Wiley and Sons, 1974, pp. 479–505.

———. "The Effects of Parental Divorce: Experiences of the Child in Later Latency." *American Journal of Orthopsychiatry.* 46 (2), April 1976, pp. 256–69.

Wheat, Ed and Wheat, Gaye. *Intended for Pleasure.* Old Tappan, New Jersey: Fleming H. Revell, 1977, 1981.

Wheat, Ed. *Sex Techniques and Sex Problems in Marriage.* A cassette program. Springdale, Arkansas: Scriptural Counsel, 1975.

Wood, Britton. *Single Adults Want to Be the Church, Too.* Nashville, Tennessee: Broadman, 1977.